It's a Wrap!

ALSO BY DIANE PHILLIPS

The Pleasure of Your Company

Keys to Successful Baking

Easy and Elegant Hors d'Oeuvres

The Perfect Mix

The Perfect Basket

It's a Wrap!

Great Meals in Small Packages

DIANE PHILLIPS

St. Martin's Griffin 🐾 *New York*

Book design by Gretchen Achilles

Library of Congress Cataloging-in-Publication Data

Phillips, Diane.
    It's a wrap / Diane Phillips.
      p.   cm.
    ISBN 0-312-16873-X
    1. Stuffed foods (Cookery)   2. Cookery, International.   I. Title.
  TX836.P48 1997
  641.8—dc21   97-17024
                                        CIP

First St. Martin's Griffin Edition: October 1997

10 9 8 7 6 5 4 3 2 1

TO LORA BRODY,

I AM BLESSED BY YOUR FRIENDSHIP.

THANKS FOR BEING THERE.

Acknowledgments

There are so many people who have encouraged me during the writing of this book, I would be remiss if I did not mention them. Hats off to Harvey White, who gave me the idea over a celebration dinner, when he said, "What's a wrap?" Thanks, Harvey. Lora Brody has been an extraordinary friend, better than I deserve. Lora, you've been an incredible source of encouragement, enthusiasm, and inspiration. Susan Ginsburg has been the agent of my dreams. Thank you, Susan, for believing in me and this project. I'm also grateful to Susan's patient assistant, John Hodgman, who always had an answer when I had a question. Heather Jackson, my editor at St. Martin's, was patient and caring during the editorial process, and her assistant, Mark Resnick, was always helpful. To all those at St. Martin's who have put so much into this book, I am deeply grateful.

While I was writing this book, my son Ryan turned sixteen and got his driver's license and my daughter Carrie turned twenty and went to Africa. Thanks, guys, the gray hairs are accumulating, but I wouldn't have had it any other way. Thanks for making it easy to be your Mom—I love you and I am so proud of both of you. To Chuck, my husband and best friend for twenty-six years of constant fun, thanks for eating all those tortillas. I promise you won't have to eat another one until we start the next book. My dear friend Chris Priebe lost his battle with cancer while I was finishing this book. Chris taught me so much about living one day at a time, and to live each day as if it were your best. I am grateful for his generosity in sharing his journey. Lastly, I want to thank all the students and friends who have been a constant source of inspiration and creativity—too many of you to name, but know that I am grateful for all you do for me each day.

Table of Contents

Introduction

From primitive Mayan kitchens to the classical dominion of Escoffier in Paris, wrapping food has been going on for centuries. Each culture and cuisine has seen the benefit of combining foods within a wrapping, then serving that package as an appetizer, main course, or dessert. Middle Easterners use lavosh, Italians encase food in bread and noodle doughs, while south-of-the-border tortillas are wrapped around tasty fillings. The Greeks stuff grape leaves and Asians have used noodle dough and seaweed wrappers to pack their foods.

Here in California, the home of the wrap, chefs are using tortillas to roll eclectic ingredients from Peking Duck to blackened fish. But these rolled tortillas do not even scratch the surface of the possibilities for wrapping foods to feed your family. Lavosh, or cracker bread, pita, phyllo, puff pastry, pasta and bread doughs, crêpes and pancakes, as well as Asian rice paper, seaweed, and noodle doughs can be used to wrap everything from appetizers to desserts. Biting into one of these wrapped creations brings an adventure in eating, with an explosion of taste in your mouth. Wraps can be picked up and eaten with your hands, or you can dig in with a knife and fork.

Why wraps? Most of us have favorite recipes to feed our families. But sometimes cooking and eating become as boring as working on an assembly line in Detroit. Not only is wrapping food fun, it will enable you to recycle leftovers, thereby saving money. Wrapping does not require expensive ingredients, and, if anything, the normal amounts of meat, chicken, or seafood are cut in half because the combination of ingredients in the wrap help to stretch your food dollar. Fillings from around the world become a vehicle to experiment with and to expand your family's culinary horizons. Think of wraps as a cultural and culinary adventure.

How do you make the best wraps? My personal opinion is that wraps benefit from contrasting textures and flavors. Wrapping Chinese chicken salad in warm flour tortillas contrasts the warmth of the tortilla with the coolness of the salad, the crunch of the vegetables with the softness of the tortilla, and the salad dressing's sweet-and-sour flavor with the bland taste of the wrapper. Each element in all of the recipes that follow has been carefully considered, then brought together to make little packages that will delight all your senses. Some would argue that the more bizarre the better when it comes to wrapping, but the combinations in this book are not out of balance; the flavors and contrasts harmonize rather than shout at you.

A small hint on lowering fat: I recommend if you are on a low-fat diet that you sauté your foods in a tiny amount of vegetable or olive oil, or with a non-stick vegetable cooking spray, thereby eliminating the cooking oil and the fat that comes with it. Substitute low-fat cheese (I don't recommend nonfat cheeses as they become rubbery when melted), low-fat sour cream, low-fat cream cheese, nonfat milk, and nonfat yogurt in recipes calling for cheese and other dairy products. When using beef, try leaner cuts, sliced thinly. Cut the amount of beef in half and double the amount of vegetables in the dish. That way the vegetables are the showcase, not the beef. Tortillas, pita, and lavosh all come in both lower fat and nonfat varieties. When using phyllo, you can cut down on the fat by spraying the phyllo with non-stick, flavored vegetable oil sprays. As with all cooking, I recommend that you eat in moderation those things that are high in fat. If you are making the Wrapped Brie with Puff Pastry, go for the gusto—there is no way to lower the fat in this one, but you don't have to eat the whole wheel by yourself, and you can use cucumber slices and carrot rounds to serve with the brie. Also, by serving your wraps as a buffet, you allow your guests to control what they put into the wrap. I feel that most entertaining is a celebration, and restrictive rules are not part of anyone's party!

When I look at recipes, I ask myself, can I find these ingredients at my local grocer? I designed this book with that in mind. If you live in an area with a full-service grocery store, you will be able to find all of the ingredients called for in these recipes. Lavosh, pita, phyllo, and tortillas were not normally found in your local grocer ten years ago, but have become as commonplace as white bread. Not only can you find these at your local market, but they now come in whole wheat, low-fat, and nonfat versions, as well as a variety of other flavors. Wraps are a great way to introduce fiber and new tastes into your family's diet without them knowing it. If you live in a town with limited access, a guide at the back of the book can direct you to excellent sources for some of the less common ingredients. Let's get wrapping!

WRAPPERS

Your local full-service grocer can supply you with most every wrap that we will use in this book. If you are having trouble finding any of the ingredients listed in the recipes, check the source guide for some of my favorite sources. Most wrappers can be found in the ethnic sections of your grocer, but if you have a limited selection, try taking a culinary field trip to grocery stores in ethnic neighborhoods for your ingredients.

Flat breads such as tortillas, lavosh, and pita will come in packages with a stamped expiration date. If you plan to use them within the time on the date stamp, these wrappers can be stored at room temperature or refrigerated in airtight storage bags. If you would prefer to freeze the wrappers, they can be frozen for up to one month, then defrosted overnight in the refrigerator before using.

Doughs such as phyllo, puff pastry, crêpes, bread doughs, and noodle wrappers can be kept refrigerated for three days, or frozen for up to two months. The doughs can be defrosted overnight in the refrigerator before rolling and wrapping.

Some wrappers can be interchanged to create a lighter, or more substantial dish. For example, wrapping dinner in leafy green vegetables rather than flat breads makes the dinner a little bit lighter, with a different style and texture. Wrapping fillings in phyllo or puff pastry makes a dramatic presentation, with delicate pastry encasing the filling. If there are fillings that you want to play with, try substituting whatever you have on hand for dinner tonight, and you may develop a new favorite for your family.

TORTILLAS

Tortillas have been a part of the South and Central American diet for centuries. Originally made with corn, they now come in a variety of flavors and colors. At my local market I can buy yellow and blue corn, flour, whole wheat, and spinach tortillas, as well as low-fat and nonfat versions. Tortillas can be used to package tacos, burritos, quesadillas, chimichangas, and a variety of nontraditional fillings. Tortillas can be kept at room temperature, or refrigerated in airtight storage bags, or frozen for future use.

LAVOSH

Lavosh, sometimes called Armenian cracker bread, comes in long sheets and can be used to wrap fillings or as a scoop for certain Middle Eastern dishes. Lavosh is made with white or whole wheat flour. It keeps, wrapped in airtight containers, at room temperature, or can be frozen for one month. Defrost the lavosh in the refrigerator overnight, if frozen, before using with your favorite wrap.

PITA

Pita, or pocket breads, come in large and small sizes; either can be used, depending on your preference. It is a flat bread with a pocket in the middle, and fillings can be spread over the bread and rolled up, or it can be cut in half, and the pockets stuffed with savory fillings.

PHYLLO

Paper-thin layers of pastry, phyllo is brushed with butter or oil to produce a flaky pastry when baked. Phyllo comes frozen in one-pound boxes at the grocery, or can be bought fresh from Greek and Armenian markets. When working with phyllo it is necessary to keep it covered with a kitchen towel to prevent it from drying out. A one-pound box of phyllo contains approximately 24 sheets that measure 14 by 18 inches. Defrost the frozen phyllo overnight in the refrigerator before using. Phyllo is prepared by brushing it with butter, and then sprinkling it with bread crumbs. The bread crumbs absorb some of the moisture in the fillings to produce a flakier pastry. If you are concerned about the amount of butter or oil that must be brushed onto the pastry, you can cut the amount by using non-stick butter or olive oil flavored cooking spray, spraying each phyllo sheet.

PUFF PASTRY

There is nothing more elegant than an appetizer, main dish, or dessert made with puff pastry. Layers of dough separated by butter rise in the oven to produce a spectacular creation. You can make your own puff pastry, or buy sheets of puff pastry in the frozen-food section of your local supermarket. Defrost the puff pastry for one hour at room temperature before using.

PASTA

Sheets of fresh pasta or large tubes of dry pasta are available at the grocery. Pastas can wrap all sorts of savory fillings and be covered with a variety of delicious sauces. Many fresh pasta shops carry flavored sheets of pasta, which make for a colorful and tasty alternative to traditional egg pastas. Store fresh pasta in the refrigerator, or freeze it for up to two months. Dry pasta keeps in a cool, dry pantry for months.

CRÊPES AND PANCAKES

Pancakes and crêpes take on a whole new look and flavor when you fill them with savory and sweet fillings for dinner and dessert. Fresh crêpes are available in the supermarket in the produce or bakery sections (see Source Guide). Making fresh crêpes is easy using a non-stick omelette pan. Stack the crêpes, separated by waxed paper, then refrigerate for two to three days, or freeze up to one month.

RICE PAPER, WONTON WRAPPERS, AND EGG ROLL WRAPPERS

Rice paper, wonton wrappers, and egg roll wrappers can be found in the Asian section of the grocery store. Wonton and egg roll wrappers can be frozen for up to two months, but I recommend you use the rice paper when it is fresh.

SEAWEED

Nori are sold in sheets at the supermarket. They are used to wrap sushi rolls and Korean beef rolls. Store unused sheets in airtight storage bags at room temperature.

BREAD DOUGHS

Food processors and bread machines make superior bread doughs in a snap. Ready to wrap in less than 60 minutes, bread can be frozen after cooking, and bread doughs keep well in the freezer for up to two months. Defrost overnight in the refrigerator before using. "Wrapped" breads, such as calzones, may be baked then frozen. Reheat in the oven before serving.

LEAFY GREEN VEGETABLES

Vegetables such as spinach, chard, lettuce, and cabbage should be washed and dried before using as "Garden" wrappers. Store in zipper-type vegetable storage bags in the vegetable crisper of your refrigerator for up to two days before using.

Rolling Your Own

THE ART OF FOLDING WRAPS

PURSE FOLDS

Purse folds make a dramatic presentation for almost any dish. Using phyllo or puff pastry with this style fold will make your wrap the center of attention at any meal. Purse folds are easy to complete, and can be refrigerated or frozen before baking.

To assemble the purse fold, center the filling on the dough. Bring two opposite corners together, then draw the other corners into the center, twisting the dough to form a topknot. Don't be afraid of twisting the dough; it will take a bit of punishment. If you are using phyllo, brush some butter over the top, or spray flavored non-stick cooking spray over it. When using puff pastry dough, paint the flat surface with an egg wash but leave the top knot untouched, as the dough will not rise as dramatically when it is washed.

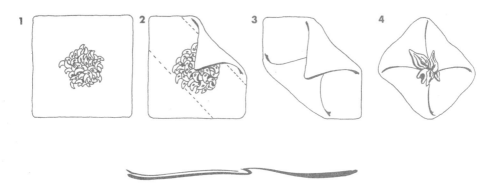

To make an egg wash whisk 1 egg and 1 tablespoon water together in a small bowl. Use the egg wash to brush onto pastry before baking. For sweet pastry, sprinkle with sugar; for savory, sprinkle with salt and fresh herbs.

CRÊPE FOLDS

This fold can be used with round wrappers like tortillas and crepes measuring approximately 6 to 8 inches. The easiest way to assemble this fold is to place the wrapper onto the serving plate. The filling is centered down the length of the wrapper, then the top and bottom are folded into the center. Generally, a crêpe fold is covered with a sauce and garnished with additional filling or fresh herbs.

1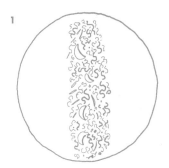

2

This fold reminds me of my Girl Scout days, when we learned to fold the flag. A fun presentation for a platter of hors d'oeuvres, this fold will put some pizazz into your wrapping repertoire. I recommend using this fold with phyllo dough, as any other wrapper would create too much dough and not enough filling. For appetizer-size pieces, you will need to cut the phyllo dough into three long pieces, measuring approximately 4½ by 6 inches. Place a tablespoon of filling at the top center of one strip of phyllo. Beginning at the top left, fold the phyllo over the filling to form a triangle. Fold the top right over the filling, and continue to fold until the strip has formed a triangle. If you decide to make larger packets, such as fruit turnovers, or larger portions of spanakopietas, cut the whole phyllo in half lengthwise, and follow the same directions for wrapping.

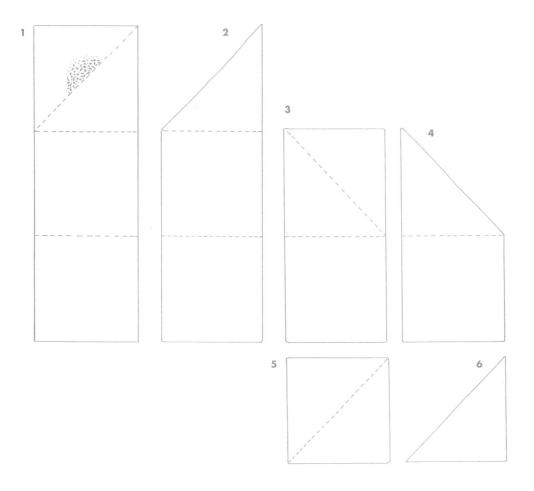

This is the typical package-type wrap. Use it for encasing filling for any type of round wrapper, as it works well with all manner of doughs. Place the wrapper onto a flat work surface. Spread the filling down the center of the wrapper. With the filling placed horizontally, fold up the bottom of the wrapper over the filling. Fold in the two sides, and then roll the bottom over the filling and tuck in the sides to form a package.

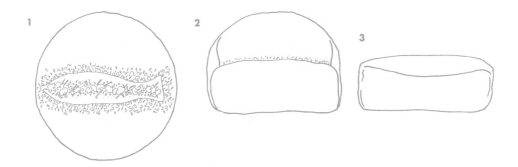

These folds are easy and result in a striking presentation for just about any wrap, with their spiral of colorful fillings. Whether you are using a round or square wrapper, these wraps will become an easy favorite. Place the wrapper onto a flat work surface and spread completely with filling. Roll the wrapper over the filling, as you would a jelly roll. Slice the roll into rounds, and bake or serve as directed.

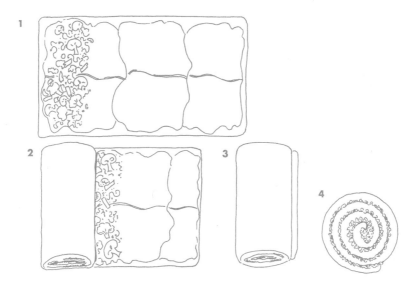

Quick as a wink, this type of wrap is generally used with a dough that needs to be baked, but can certainly be used with tortillas for making quesadillas, or with bread dough for calzone. Place the dough on a flat work surface, then arrange the filling on one half of the dough. Fold the other half of the dough over the filling and crimp the edges with the tines of a fork, or with a ravioli cutter, to make an attractive border. Follow the same directions for tortillas, but there is no need to crimp the edges to seal the dough.

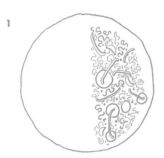
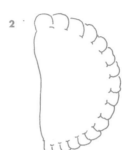

This traditional fold, used for wrapping Chinese noodle dough into an egg roll, is also used for any other rectangular-type wrapper. Place the wrapper onto a flat work surface, then place the filling at the short end. Fold the top of the wrapper over the filling, then fold in the sides, and continue to roll the wrapper until it is complete. This works well with lavosh, phyllo, puff pastry, and noodle doughs.

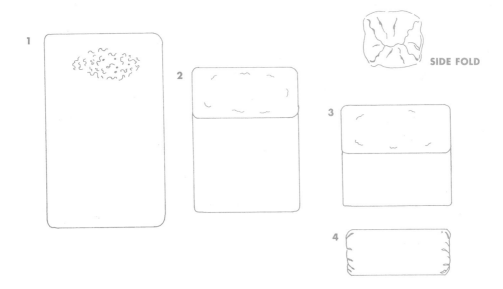

SIDE FOLD

Stocking the Pantry

A well-stocked pantry can mean the difference between a home-cooked meal and take-out food. If there isn't anything in your pantry, your imagination has nowhere to run. Being prepared is good for those of us who have a tendency to be in a rush and are unable to think of "what's for dinner" the minute we get home from work. These are a few of the essentials that I think keep you prepared for eating well and wrapping up a great dinner.

Some of us do not have enough freezer or pantry space to keep a large stockpile of ingredients. I would advise you to look at your space, look at the recipes that appeal to you in this book, and then decide which ingredients you are most likely to use. Remember who you are cooking for—not every five-year-old is wild about black beans or sun-dried tomatoes. I have a friend whose children think they don't like sun-dried tomatoes, but because she purees the tomatoes, they can't be detected. Keep in mind that it is perfectly acceptable to leave out an ingredient your family isn't crazy about, or to serve that ingredient on the side, if that's possible. Not everyone has a taste for goat cheese and pâté, so keep it simple and you won't have any disappointments. The more you have to choose from, the more likely you will be to make dinner than to call for a pizza.

Spices are a cook's arsenal. They provide the pizazz for simple meals, turning them into extraordinary dishes. Make sure that you keep on hand spices that you will actually use. Some of you may still have the paprika that you got with the spice rack from your wedding shower twelve years ago. My advice is to go through your spice cabinet and throw out any spice jars that are old. You'll know the ones—the metal is starting to rust if it's a can, or when you remove the top, the spice doesn't have any fragrance whatsoever. Paprika is susceptible to getting small weevils, so check the spices and dispose of any that contain weevils. I like to use dehydrated spices in soups and stews because when they are rehydrated they regain their bright green color, and immediately infuse dishes with the perfume of the spice. I do not recommend buying ground spices because they lose a lot of their oils when they are ground. Instead, look for the word "whole" on the spice jar. These are a selection of the spices I keep on hand.

BAY LEAVES	**POPPY SEEDS**
CAJUN SEASONING	**ROSEMARY**
CURRY POWDER	**SEA SALT OR KOSHER SALT**
DILL WEED	**SESAME SEEDS**
GREEK OREGANO	**SWEET BASIL**
GREEK SEASONING	**WHOLE BLACK PEPPERCORNS**
GROUND CINNAMON	**WHOLE THYME LEAVES**
LEMON PEPPER	

Fresh herbs vs. dried herbs: Fresh herbs bring a delicate flavor to dishes that are not simmered for a long time. If you are simmering a dish for more than 20 minutes, I would recommend a dried herb. Heartier soups, stews, and vegetable ragouts are really enhanced by the powerful flavor of dried herbs. Delicate salads and uncooked sauces and salsas benefit from fresh herbs. I particularly like to use dehydrated herbs rather than commercially dried herbs. When rehydrated, they regain some of their original color, and impart a closer flavor to their fresh counterpart.

CAPERS

CHEDDAR CHEESE

FROZEN CHICKEN (PREFERABLY BONELESS)

FROZEN CORN, AND OTHER FROZEN VEG-
ETABLES, SUCH AS FROZEN PETITE-SIZE
PEAS AND CHOPPED SPINACH

FROZEN PEELED AND DEVEINED RAW
SHRIMP

GRANNY SMITH APPLES

NONFAT YOGURT

PACKAGED SALAD GREENS

PARMESAN CHEESE; SMALL CHUNKS FOR
GRATING OR FRESHLY GRATED FROM THE
MARKET

PESTO IN A TUBE

PHYLLO DOUGH

PUFF PASTRY SHEETS

SOUR CREAM

TORTILLAS

DRY PANTRY

BREAD CRUMBS

CAJUN SEASONING

CANNED ARTICHOKE HEARTS

CANNED BEANS (KEEP A VARIETY:
GARBANZO, BLACK, KIDNEY, PINTO)

CANNED CHOPPED TOMATOES

CANNED NUTS

CANNED STOCK (CHICKEN, BEEF, AND
VEGETABLE)

CHOCOLATE CHIPS

COCOA POWDER

DIJON MUSTARD

DRIED OR DEHYDRATED SPICES (SEE ABOVE)

DRIED PASTAS (LOTS OF DIFFERENT SHAPES)

FRESH GARLIC

LAVOSH (FREEZE IF NOT USING
IMMEDIATELY)

NORI

OLIVE OIL

ONIONS (RED AND YELLOW)

ORZO

PITA BREADS

POTATOES (RED AND RUSSET)

RICE

RICE WINE VINEGAR

SESAME OIL

SOY SAUCE

SUN-DRIED TOMATOES

TABASCO (RED AND GREEN VARIETIES)

TOMATO PASTE IN TUBES

WORCESTERSHIRE SAUCE

Dried bay leaves are an excellent natural pesticide for the pantry. Scatter several leaves on your pantry shelves, and stick a bay leaf into flours and cornmeal, and around boxes of dried pasta. This retards the hatching of weevils in the flour, and does not affect the flavor.

Wrappetizers

Served with drinks before dinner, or as a buffet assortment, wrappetizers are wonderful conversation builders. They provide the perfect one or two bites that will curb appetites as a prelude to dinner. An around the world culinary journey, this chapter has selections from Greek Spanakopitas to Japanese Gyoza. These wraps from a global pantry are easy to make and will enhance any predinner cocktail hour.

Fresh spinach, pea pods, and basil all provide lower-fat alternatives to wrap with than phyllo and other doughs. When serving appetizers, I generally select one hot and one cold, or one healthy alternative as well as a splurge. All the appetizers in this chapter can be made ahead of time, and refrigerated or frozen until ready to serve. Wraps like California Rolls, Sushi Wraps, and Johnnycakes become the party when your guest can roll their own. Set out all the ingredients on a counter or buffet table, provide plates, and then allow your guests to pick the filling they'd like to wrap. This not only gets the conversation going, it gives new meaning to the phrase "Playing with your food."

Bacon Wraps

Basil-Wrapped Scallop Seviche

California Rolls

Chicken and Vegetable Gyoza

Crab Wraps

Cucumber Wraps

Curried Mushroom Rolls

Italian Roll-ups

Jammin' PB&J Wraps

Jicama Sticks

Johnnycakes with Smoked Salmon
and Capers

Mexicana Tortilla Rolls

Oriental Chicken and
Spinach Wraps

Parmesan Bruschetta

Pea Pod Wraps

Prosciutto Palmiers

Prosciutto-Wrapped Strawberries

Spanakopitas

Sushi Rolls

Thai Spring Rolls

Wrapped Brie with Apricots and
Dried Cranberries

Bacon Wraps

Bacon has gotten a bad "rap" in the past few years, and although I do not eat a lot of bacon, it does add flavor to many dishes and makes a terrific wrapper. If for dietary reasons you cannot eat pork, turkey bacons found in the supermarket are an excellent alternative to pork. These wrappetizers are simple, can be made the day before, and take only a brief warm-up in the microwave or conventional oven before serving.

10 STRIPS BACON, EACH CUT INTO THIRDS

1/4 CUP DIJON MUSTARD

1/2 CUP MAJOR GREY'S CHUTNEY

30 WHOLE WATER CHESTNUTS

Lay 1 strip of bacon (cut into thirds) on a cutting board. In a small bowl, combine the mustard and chutney. Spread a small amount of the mixture over each piece of bacon. Set a water chestnut at the end of the bacon strip, and roll the bacon over the water chestnut to make a tight ball. Repeat until all 30 wraps are assembled. Place 10 wraps on a microwavable plate covered with paper toweling. Microwave on High for 5 minutes. At this point the bacon should be just about done. Remove the wraps from the plate and place on another plate, refrigerating until just before you are ready to serve them. Remicrowave the bacon wraps for 1 to 2 minutes on 50% power, or until they are crisp. Drain and serve with toothpicks.

If you do not own a microwave, preheat the broiler for 10 minutes. Place all the bacon wraps on a broiler pan, and broil 4 inches away from the heat until the bacon just begins to crisp, about 6 minutes, turning halfway to brown evenly. Remove from the oven and serve or refrigerate. When ready to serve, warm in a preheated 400°F oven for 15 minutes.

Basil-Wrapped Scallop Seviche

SERVES 10 TO 12

A twist on traditional seviche, this light starter is low in fat and high in taste. The scallops "cook" in lime juice and seasonings for a few hours in the refrigerator, then are wrapped in colorful fresh basil leaves, speared with a toothpick, and served cold. For a rainbow effect, try to find opal basil, which has a gorgeous purple color and more of a licorice taste than green.

1 POUND FRESH SEA SCALLOPS

1/2 CUP FRESH LIME JUICE

1/2 CUP CHOPPED RED ONION

1/4 CUP CHOPPED FRESH PARSLEY

1/4 CUP VEGETABLE OIL

1/2 TEASPOON DRIED OREGANO, OR
1 TABLESPOON CHOPPED FRESH OREGANO

1/2 TEASPOON SALT

1/4 TEASPOON WHITE PEPPER

DASH OF TABASCO

2 BUNCHES FRESH BASIL (ABOUT
40 LEAVES), WASHED AND DRIED

Cut each scallop in half. In a medium glass mixing bowl, blend the lime juice and the remaining seasonings with a whisk. Add the scallops, and cover the bowl with plastic wrap. Refrigerate for 4 to 6 hours. Drain the scallops. Place a basil leaf on a cutting board or flat surface, then take a scallop and place it at the end of the leaf. Roll the leaf around the scallop and secure it with a toothpick. Continue until all the scallops are wrapped. Chill the scallops, or serve immediately. Garnish the platter with bouquets of fresh herbs and lime wedges.

Fresh basil is fragile and keeps only a short period of time in the refrigerator. Store it as you would salad greens, but if you cannot use it at its peak, pack it into a 2-cup glass jar, cover it with olive oil (not extra-virgin), and refrigerate. When you need to use fresh basil in a recipe, remove the basil from the oil and add it to the dish. The oil also takes on the flavor of the basil and you can use it in salad dressings, or to brush on foccaccia bread.

California Rolls

SERVES 10 TO 12

Not the traditional sushi roll, these California Rolls are rolled tortillas spread with black beans, then the filling ingredients are lined up on the tortillas to form a beautiful mosaic of colors and tastes. Black beans not only add spice and color, they become the "glue" that holds the rolls together. These pretty rolls make a stunning addition to any party tray.

6 FLOUR TORTILLAS (12-INCH)

1 CUP BLACK BEANS OLÉ (SEE RECIPE, PAGE 25)

1½ CUPS GRATED COLBY/JACK CHEESE

½ CUP CHOPPED FRESH CILANTRO

½ CUP CHOPPED FRESH SCALLIONS (GREEN ONIONS)

½ CUP DICED CUCUMBER

1 CUP CHOPPED FRESH TOMATOES

3-OUNCE PACKAGE CREAM CHEESE, CUT INTO ½-INCH CUBES

1 CUP COOKED BEEF FAJITAS (SEE RECIPE, PAGE 91)

Place a sheet of plastic wrap 1½ times the size of the tortilla on a flat work surface or cutting board. Center the tortilla on the plastic wrap and spread a thin layer of the black beans over the surface of the tortilla. Working in rows, from the bottom of the tortilla, make lines of cheese, cilantro, scallion, cucumber, tomato, cream cheese, and beef. Using the plastic wrap as a guide, begin at the bottom of the tortilla and roll it tightly. Twist the ends of the plastic wrap to seal, and refrigerate for at least 1 hour. Repeat with the remaining tortillas. When ready to serve, unwrap the plastic and slice the tortilla into 1-inch rounds. Place the California Rolls on a platter, garnished with fresh cilantro and a bowl of Fresh Tomato Salsa (see page 38 for recipe) for dipping.

Black Beans Olé

If you have the time, I recommend using dried black beans, which generally need to be soaked overnight before cooking. There are two ways to prepare black beans for cooking. The first is to soak the beans in water to cover them overnight, discard the water, and cook the beans in fresh water to cover for 1 hour until tender. Another, faster way is to bring water and beans to a boil for 2 minutes. Allow to soak in the water for 1 hour. Drain and discard the water. You are then ready to cook with the beans. Some beans do not have to be soaked at all, so check the package for soaking/cooking instructions. If you are using canned black beans, make sure to drain and rinse them before using.

1 TABLESPOON VEGETABLE OIL

1 LARGE ONION, CHOPPED

2 CLOVES GARLIC, MINCED

1¹/₂ TEASPOONS GROUND CUMIN

¹/₂ TEASPOON DRIED OREGANO

1 TABLESPOON FINELY CHOPPED HOT CHILIES (OPTIONAL)

1 CUP CHOPPED FRESH TOMATOES

2 CANS (19-OUNCE) BLACK BEANS, DRAINED AND RINSED

¹/₄ CUP RED WINE

SALT AND PEPPER, TO TASTE

In a large sauté pan, heat the oil over medium heat and add the onion, garlic, spices, and chilies (if used). Sauté the mixture until the onions become soft and translucent. Stir in the tomatoes, and cook an additional 3 to 4 minutes. Add the black beans and the red wine, cooking until the beans become very soft and begin to break up. This should take about 10 minutes. Season with salt and pepper to taste. The beans will keep refrigerated for 5 days. To soften the beans for spreading, reheat in the microwave, or over low heat on the stove top.

Chicken and Vegetable Gyoza

SERVES 10 TO 12

The Japanese cousin to Chinese pot stickers, these delicious dumplings are loaded with chicken and vegetables. They can be steamed, or browned in oil, then cooked in chicken broth until the liquid is absorbed. Either way, they are tasty treats for lunch or a prelude for dinner. Joyce Chen products sell a nifty little press that will crimp the edges of the gyoza for you in one step. Otherwise, enlist the help of your spouse or children to help you seal each dumpling. Gyoza dough is found in the refrigerated pasta or Asian noodle section of your grocer.

1 WHOLE CHICKEN BREAST, BONED, SKINNED, AND FINELY MINCED

1 PACKAGE (10 OUNCES) FROZEN CHOPPED SPINACH, DEFROSTED AND SQUEEZED OF ALL MOISTURE

$^1/_2$ CUP GRATED CARROT

1 TABLESPOON SOY SAUCE

1 TABLESPOON SESAME OIL

1 TEASPOON SHERRY

1 TEASPOON CORNSTARCH

1 SCALLION (GREEN ONION), MINCED

1 TABLESPOON MINCED FRESH GINGER

1 TEASPOON SALT

1 PACKAGE GYOZA WRAPPERS

2 TABLESPOONS OIL

2 CUPS CHICKEN BROTH

In a large bowl, combine the chicken, spinach, carrot, and seasonings. Using a tablespoon, or small scoop, place 1 tablespoon of this filling in the center of a gyoza wrapper. Fold the dough over the filling, pinching together just the top to make a half circle. On the side nearest you, form 2 to 3 pleats on each side with a fork, then pinch them to meet the opposite side and seal. If you have a gyoza maker, place the wrapper in the gyoza press, arrange a tablespoon of filling to the center, close the press, and remove the gyoza. At this point, the gyoza may be refrigerated, or frozen for later use.

To serve, heat 2 tablespoons of vegetable oil in a 12-inch, heavy nonstick skillet over medium-high heat. Lightly brown the gyoza until golden on the bottom, pour in 1 cup of the chicken broth, and cover the skillet. Cover and cook over medium heat until most of the liquid is absorbed. Uncover and continue cooking until the liquid is completely absorbed, and the Gyoza is golden-brown. Cook the remaining gyoza in the same manner.

To steam the gyoza, heat the 2 cups of chicken broth in a steamer. Place the gyoza on the steamer rack and steam for 30 minutes. Serve with the following dipping sauce.

Dipping Sauce

$1/4$ CUP SOY SAUCE

2 TABLESPOONS SESAME OIL

1 TABLESPOON RICE VINEGAR

1 SCALLION (GREEN ONION), CHOPPED

2 CLOVES GARLIC, MINCED

Mix the dipping sauce ingredients together and serve in a shallow dish when combined.

Crab Wraps

Another show stopper, these rolls with their delectable crabmeat filling will garner rave reviews from your guests. If you are serving these with other phyllo appetizers you may want to vary their shape. Rather than triangles, you may want to use the "egg roll" wrap technique. Either way, these are heaven in a bite. If you cannot find crab at your market, or it may break the bank, feel free to substitute an equal amount of cooked shrimp, chopped finely.

1 TABLESPOON BUTTER

$1/2$ CUP FINELY CHOPPED MUSHROOMS

$1/4$ CUP CHOPPED SCALLIONS (GREEN ONIONS)

1 CUP COOKED AND FLAKED FRESH CRABMEAT

1 CUP SHREDDED MONTEREY JACK CHEESE

A 3-OUNCE PACKAGE CREAM CHEESE, SOFTENED

$1/3$ CUP MAYONNAISE

2 TABLESPOONS MINCED FRESH PARSLEY

1 TEASPOON PREPARED HORSERADISH

1 TEASPOON WORCESTERSHIRE SAUCE

$1/2$ POUND PHYLLO DOUGH

1 CUP (2 STICKS) BUTTER, MELTED AND COOLED

$1/2$ TO 1 CUP BREAD CRUMBS

Melt the butter in a skillet, adding the mushrooms, scallions, and crab. Sauté until the mushroom liquid is absorbed. Allow to cool. In a medium mixing bowl, blend the Monterey Jack cheese, cream cheese, mayonnaise, parsley, horseradish, and Worcestershire sauce. Add the crab mixture, stirring well to blend. You may refrigerate the filling at this point, until you are ready to wrap.

Place the phyllo on a flat work surface, and cover it with a kitchen towel. Remove 1 sheet of phyllo, brush it with butter, and then sprinkle with bread crumbs. Cut the phyllo into 3 equal pieces, lengthwise. Place 1 tablespoon of the filling at the top center of the strip. Fold over the top, then fold in the sides. Brush the sides with the melted butter, and roll the phyllo into a neat package. Brush again with butter, and transfer to a cookie sheet that has been lined with parchment or buttered aluminum foil. Continue to roll the phyllo until you've used up all the filling. Refrigerate or freeze the rolls until ready to serve. When ready to cook, preheat the oven to 350°F and bake the rolls for 20 minutes, or until golden-brown. If the phyllo has been frozen, bake the rolls frozen, extending the cooking time 7 to 10 minutes.

*Buying that bunch of **fresh parsley** seemed like a good idea at the time, but it doesn't stay fresh for very long. After you have washed the parsley, dry it thoroughly and then process it with the metal blade of the food processor, until it is chopped. Place it in a zipper-type storage bag and freeze. You can use it right out of the bag.*

Cucumber Wraps

SERVES 10 TO 12

A whole cucumber stuffed with a spread made from Boursin cheese and smoked salmon, then sliced into rounds, reveals a beautiful pattern of green, pink, and white. These wraps are easy to assemble, and can be made a day ahead.

8 OUNCES BOURSIN OR OTHER GARLIC HERB CHEESE

1/4 POUND SMOKED SALMON (DO NOT USE LOX)

1 HOT HOUSE CUCUMBER

SPRIGS OF FRESH DILL OR PARSLEY FOR GARNISH

Blend the Boursin with the smoked salmon and set aside. Cut off the ends of the cucumber and then cut the cucumber into 3-inch lengths. Hollow out the inside and discard seeds. Stuff the cucumber with the cheese/salmon mixture. Wrap the cucumber in plastic wrap and refrigerate overnight. When ready to serve, cut the cucumber into 1-inch rounds. Garnish each with a sprig of fresh dill or parsley.

Hot house cucumbers are a smart buy at the grocer's. Although they may cost a bit more, they are longer than the waxed variety of cucumber, seedless, and the skin is edible. The result is more usable cucumber for Wrappetizers or salads.

Curried Mushroom Rolls

SERVES 10 TO 12 (36 TO 48 PIECES)

Spicy and exotic, these wraps are encased in flaky, buttery phyllo and provide a perfect foil for that glass of wine before dinner. Feel free to substitute other types of mushrooms for the filling. Try using shiitakes, crimini, or a combination of all three for an unusual taste.

4 TABLESPOONS ($\frac{1}{2}$ STICK) BUTTER

1 POUND WHITE MUSHROOMS, CHOPPED

$\frac{1}{2}$ CUP FINELY CHOPPED SCALLIONS (GREEN ONIONS)

3 TABLESPOONS FLOUR

$\frac{1}{2}$ TEASPOON SALT

$\frac{1}{2}$ TEASPOON CURRY POWDER

$\frac{1}{4}$ CUP HEAVY CREAM

$\frac{1}{2}$ POUND PHYLLO DOUGH

1 CUP (2 STICKS) BUTTER, MELTED AND COOLED

$\frac{1}{2}$ CUP TO 1 CUP DRY UNFLAVORED BREAD CRUMBS

Melt the butter in a 10-inch skillet or sauté pan. Add the mushrooms and scallions, cooking until the mushrooms are softened. Reduce the heat to low, stir in the flour, salt, and curry powder, stirring until thickened. Add the cream and cook until bubbly. Remove from the heat, and cool in the refrigerator until ready to use.

Place the phyllo on a flat surface, and cover with a kitchen towel. Remove 1 sheet of phyllo, brush generously with melted butter, and sprinkle with bread crumbs. Cut the phyllo into 3 equal pieces, lengthwise. Place 1 tablespoon of filling at the top of the strip. Fold the top left corner over the filling to form a triangle, then fold the top right over the filling, and continue to fold until the packet is complete. Brush with butter and transfer to a cookie sheet lined with parchment or buttered aluminum foil. Refrigerate or freeze until ready to use. When ready to serve, bake the rolls in a preheated 350-degree oven for 10 to 15 minutes, or until they are golden-brown. If the rolls have been frozen, bake them (still frozen) for an additional 7 to 10 minutes.

Italian Roll-ups

SERVES 12

Another variation on the pinwheel wrap theme, this time using lavosh, these colorful rolls are reminiscent of the Italian flag with red sun-dried tomatoes, dark green pesto, and the creamy smooth garlic-flavored white cream cheese. Adding pine nuts and shredded Provolone cheese takes these wraps to another level. Adding $^1/_4$ pound thinly sliced prosciutto makes a mouthwatering rolled sandwich.

2 SHEETS LAVOSH

2 PACKAGES (8-OUNCE) CREAM CHEESE, SOFTENED

1 TEASPOON CRUSHED GARLIC

1 TEASPOON WORCESTERSHIRE SAUCE

1 CUP SUN-DRIED TOMATOES, PACKED IN OIL, DRAINED, AND SLICED

1 CUP BASIL PESTO (SEE RECIPE, PAGE 124)

$^1/_2$ CUP PINE NUTS (PIGNOLI)

1 CUP GRATED PROVOLONE CHEESE

CHOPPED FRESH PARSLEY AND BASIL FOR GARNISH

Spread the lavosh on a cutting board or flat work surface. In a small bowl, cream together the cream cheese, garlic, and Worcestershire sauce. Spread a thin layer of cream cheese over a sheet of lavosh, then spread a thin layer of the Basil Pesto over the cream cheese. Sprinkle with sun-dried tomatoes, pine nuts, and Provolone. Repeat with the remaining lavosh. Roll up the lavosh from the long end, cut off 2 inches from the ends (these usually do not get as much filling and can be discarded, or eaten by the cook). Wrap the rolls in plastic wrap and refrigerate for 2 hours or overnight. Slice into 2-inch rounds and serve. Garnish the platter with chopped fresh parsley and basil.

Jammin' PB&J Wraps

SERVES 6 TO 8

Bringing children of all ages into the kitchen is always fun—and usually messy. These wraps are a surefire recipe for excitement in the kitchen. Provide each person with a tortilla, then place all the ingredients on the counter for them to create their own master-pieces. This is the one time when you can't tell your children to stop playing with their food!

12 FLOUR TORTILLAS (12-INCH)

1 JAR (16 OUNCES) CREAMY PEANUT BUTTER

1 JAR (16 OUNCES) CHUNKY PEANUT BUTTER

2 CUPS RAISINS

3 CUPS CHOCOLATE CHIP MORSELS

6 BANANAS, SLICED

2 CUPS MINIATURE MARSHMALLOWS

2 CUPS CHOPPED PEANUTS

1 CUP FLAKED COCONUT

2 CUPS SLICED APPLES, SPRINKLED WITH LEMON JUICE TO PRESERVE THEIR COLOR

2 CUPS STRAWBERRY JAM

Each person takes a tortilla and spreads the peanut butter of choice over the tortilla. Have each person select their fillings, slicing the bananas just before they are placed on the tortilla. Roll up each tortilla, and slice into 4 equal pieces.

Jicama Sticks

Jicama is a root vegetable that adds a sweet apple-like crispness to salads and raw vegetable dishes. Pairing jicama with crispy bacon provides a delicious prelude to dinner. These wraps can be prepared two days ahead of time, and then require a brief zap in the microwave or broiler before serving.

10 STRIPS BACON, EACH CUT INTO THREE PIECES

1/4 CUP DIJON MUSTARD

1/2 CUP BROWN SUGAR

30 STICKS JICAMA, CUT INTO 1/2 X 4-INCH STICKS

Lay the bacon on a cutting board. In a small bowl, combine the mustard with the brown sugar. Spread some mixture over each bacon slice, and then twist each around a jicama stick. Lay the sticks on a microwavable plate covered with paper toweling. Microwave 10 sticks at a time, on High, for 5 minutes. Repeat until all 30 sticks are done. Refrigerate until ready to serve. When ready to serve, reheat at 50% power for 3 to 5 minutes. If you don't have a microwave, preheat the broiler for 10 minutes. Arrange the Jicama Sticks on a broiler pan. Broil 3 minutes on each side, or until the bacon is crisp. Serve immediately.

Johnnycakes with Smoked Salmon and Capers

SERVES 8

Originally, Johnnycakes were small cornmeal loaves made by the pioneers to take on their journeys. In New England, Johnnycakes have taken on the appearance of cornmeal pancakes. Thin and crisp, served with apple butter or syrup, they make a delightful breakfast. But when served with smoked salmon and crème fraîche they become a most elegant way to begin a meal. This makes a wonderful crowd pleaser when you place all the ingredients out on a counter and have your guests roll their own. If you are pulling out all the stops, you should include a small bowl of caviar to make small caviar cakes as well.

JOHNNYCAKE BATTER

2 EGGS

1 1/2 CUPS MILK

1/2 TEASPOON SALT

2 TABLESPOONS MELTED BUTTER

1 CUP YELLOW CORNMEAL

1 CUP ALL-PURPOSE FLOUR

2 TEASPOONS BAKING POWDER

NONSTICK OIL OR BUTTER SPRAY

In a medium mixing bowl, whisk together the eggs and milk. Gradually add the salt, butter, cornmeal, flour, and baking powder. Heat a griddle or nonstick skillet, then lightly grease with nonstick spray. Using about 2 tablespoons of batter for each cake, pour 4 small cakes into the griddle. When bubbles begin to form on the top of the cakes, turn them over. Cook an additional 2 minutes, or until brown on both sides. Remove to a serving platter.

Crème Fraîche

This recipe is so easy, and the results are phenomenal. For a spur of the moment substitute, use 1 cup sour cream that has been thinned with 2 tablespoons heavy whipping cream for the ingredients listed below.

1 CUP HEAVY WHIPPING CREAM   2 TABLESPOONS BUTTERMILK

Combine the cream and buttermilk in a glass jar with a screw top. Shake the mixture and allow to sit at room temperature for 24 to 36 hours, or until thickened to the consistency of sour cream. Refrigerate until ready to serve.

ASSEMBLY

30 JOHNNYCAKES

1 CUP CRÈME FRAÎCHE

$^1/_2$ POUND SMOKED SALMON, THINLY SLICED

$^1/_2$ CUP CAPERS, DRAINED

$^1/_2$ CUP CHOPPED RED ONION FOR GARNISH

$^1/_4$ CUP CHOPPED FRESH PARSLEY FOR GARNISH

Place a Johnnycake on the serving platter. Spread a small amount of Crème Fraîche on each cake, top with a small piece of smoked salmon and a caper. Fold the cake in half. Arrange all the Johnnycakes on the serving platter, and garnish with red onion and chopped parsley.

Mexicana Tortilla Rolls

SERVES 12

These wraps are almost like peanuts, they are so addictive. Tortillas are rolled around a spicy Southwestern filling and then cut into pinwheel-shaped appetizers. Serve with an assortment of rolled wraps, then just sit back and watch the compliments fly! Make sure to garnish this dish with lime wedges, chopped cilantro, and hot peppers, as well as Guacamole and Fresh Tomato Salsa (see pages 38 and 39 for recipes). Flavored tortillas will add interesting flavor and color to these wraps.

8 OUNCES SOFTENED CREAM CHEESE

8 OUNCES SOUR CREAM

1 CUP GRATED CHEDDAR CHEESE

½ CUP ROASTED GREEN CHILIES, CHOPPED

¼ CUP CHOPPED BLACK OLIVES

4 SCALLIONS (GREEN ONIONS), CHOPPED

¼ CUP CHOPPED RED PEPPER

2 TABLESPOONS CHOPPED FRESH CILANTRO

6 FLOUR TORTILLAS (10–12 INCH)

FOR GARNISH:

GUACAMOLE (PAGE 39)

FRESH TOMATO SALSA (PAGE 38)

LIME WEDGES

1 BUNCH CHOPPED FRESH CILANTRO

Cream the sour cream and cream cheese together until smooth. Add the remaining cheddar, chilies, olives, scallions, red pepper, and cilantro. Spread a layer of the mixture onto each tortilla, then roll up tightly. Wrap in foil or plastic and refrigerate several hours, or overnight. Just before serving, cut into slices about 1 inch thick. Serve with Guacamole and Fresh Tomato Salsa, and garnish with lime wedges and additional chopped cilantro.

Leftover tortillas can be sprinkled with salsa and grated cheese, and then baked for a quick Mexican pizza.

Fresh Tomato Salsa

Everyone has a favorite salsa recipe, and this one is mine. I may change my mind with the next salsa I try, but this one is simple to prepare and the ingredients are easy to find.

4 CUPS CHOPPED FRESH TOMATOES, DRAINED

$^1/_3$ CUP TOMATO PUREE

$^1/_4$ CUP FINELY CHOPPED ONION

2 GARLIC CLOVES, MINCED

2 JALAPEÑO CHILI PEPPERS, SEEDED AND MINCED

2 TABLESPOONS CHOPPED FRESH CILANTRO

1 TABLESPOON CHOPPED FRESH OREGANO (OR 1 TEASPOON DRIED)

1 TEASPOON SALT

2 TABLESPOONS LIME JUICE

Combine all the ingredients in a glass bowl, and refrigerate for 6 hours. If you desire a less chunky salsa, run this through a blender or food processor until smooth.

Guacamole

MAKES 2 CUPS

There must be hundreds of recipes for guacamole, and I like them all. This is a basic recipe that you can adjust any way you like. To retard discoloration of the avocados, make sure that you mix in a bit of lime or lemon juice. I like to use the Haas variety of avocado, the one with the dark pebbly exterior.

2 LARGE, FULLY RIPENED AVOCADOS, PEELED, PIT REMOVED

¹/₄ CUP DICED TOMATO

1 CHOPPED SCALLION (GREEN ONION)

1 TEASPOON FRESH LIME JUICE

1 TABLESPOON FRESH TOMATO SALSA (PAGE 38)

1 GARLIC CLOVE, MINCED

¹/₂ TEASPOON SALT

Mash the avocados in a mixing bowl. Add the remaining ingredients and stir until blended. Serve immediately, or cover with plastic wrap and refrigerate until ready to serve. To prevent discoloration while the dip is in the refrigerator, spread a bit more lime juice over the top of the guacamole.

Oriental Chicken and Spinach Wraps

SERVE 8 TO 10

Golden morsels of chicken nestled inside gorgeous, dark green spinach leaves and served with a sesame yogurt dipping sauce make an elegant and colorful beginning to any meal. The chicken and the dipping sauce may be prepared a day ahead of time and refrigerated until ready to serve.

CHICKEN

2 CUPS CHICKEN BROTH

1/4 CUP SOY SAUCE

2 WHOLE CHICKEN BREASTS, SKINNED AND BONED

Combine the chicken broth and soy sauce in a 3-quart skillet and bring the liquid to a boil. Add the chicken breasts, turn the heat down, and simmer for 10 to 15 minutes, until the chicken is tender. Cool and cut the chicken into bite-size chunks.

SPINACH

1 POUND FRESH SPINACH, WASHED, STEMS REMOVED

Place 10 to 12 spinach leaves on a microwavable plate. Microwave on high for 20 seconds, or until the leaves are pliable. If you don't have a microwave, bring 6 cups of water to a boil. Place the spinach in a colander in the sink. Pour the water over the spinach, drain then plunge the spinach into cold water. Drain the spinach and pat dry. Cool before rolling the leaves.

ASSEMBLY

SPINACH LEAVES

CHICKEN CHUNKS

Place a spinach leaf on a work surface, then place a piece of chicken in its center. Fold the bottom of the spinach leaf over the chicken piece, fold in the sides, and roll the chicken toward the top to enclose it. Skewer with a toothpick, and refrigerate until ready to serve. Serve with Dipping Sauce.

Dipping Sauce

1 CUP SOUR CREAM OR NONFAT YOGURT   2 TEASPOONS SOY SAUCE

2 TABLESPOONS SESAME SEEDS   1 TEASPOON SESAME OIL

1 TEASPOON GRATED GINGER

Combine all the ingredients in a small glass bowl. Refrigerate for at least 3 hours before serving.

Parmesan Bruschetta

SERVES 6 TO 8

Traditional bruschetta are small pieces of twice-toasted bread that have been spread with savory fillings. Our "wrapped" Parmesan Bruschetta are small wafers made from Parmesan cheese, sandwiched with savory fillings, and served as a first course—or they can be floated in soup. The Parmesan wafers should be made from the best-quality cheese. You will also need a heavy skillet with a non-stick coating to properly prepare these tasty wrappetizers. The pestos are delicious over hot pasta, too.

1 CUP BEST-QUALITY IMPORTED PARMESAN CHEESE, GRATED (I LOVE PARMIGIANA REGGIANO)

Heat an 8- or 10-inch non-stick skillet over medium-high heat. Place 3 to 4 single layers of 1¹/₂ tablespoons cheese, measuring about 2 inches in diameter in the skillet. As the cheese cooks, it will firm. Turn the cheese when the edges begin to turn golden, and cook the other side. Remove the wafers to a plate covered with paper towels. When all the wafers are done, place the wafers on a cutting board or flat work surface. Spread 1 tablespoon each of Sun-dried Tomato Pesto or Artichoke-Heart Pesto (recipes follow) on each bruschetta and cover with another. Serve at room temperature.

*Making your own **sun-dried tomatoes** is easy and economical. Buy dried tomatoes at the grocer, then layer them in a jar with oil, slivers of garlic, fresh parsley, and basil. Allow tomatoes to soften in the oil for at least 24 hours before using. Refrigerate until ready to use.*

Sun-dried Tomato Pesto

$1/2$ CUP SUN-DRIED TOMATOES, PACKED IN OIL, DRAINED

3 CLOVES GARLIC

$1/4$ CUP OLIVE OIL

2 TABLESPOONS BALSAMIC VINEGAR

$1/2$ CUP FRESH BASIL LEAVES

$1/2$ CUP FRESHLY GRATED PARMESAN CHEESE

Combine all the ingredients in the work bowl of a food processor. Process for 15 seconds. Scrape down the bowl, and process for 20 more seconds. Remove the pesto from the bowl, and store in a glass jar in the refrigerator for one month, or freeze for up to 2 months.

Artichoke-Heart Pesto

2 ($4^1/_2$-OUNCE) JARS MARINATED ARTICHOKE HEARTS, DRAINED, RESERVING THE LIQUID

2 CLOVES GARLIC

$1/2$ CUP PINE NUTS (PIGNOLI)

$1/2$ CUP GRATED PARMESAN CHEESE

Combine all the ingredients in the work bowl of a food processor. Process the mixture for 25 seconds. Scrape the bowl, adding one to two tablespoons of reserve liquid if the pesto seems dry. Process for 15 additional seconds. Remove pesto and store in the refrigerator until ready to use. Artichoke-Heart Pesto keeps in the refrigerator for 2 weeks, or frozen for up to 2 months.

Pea Pod Wraps

SERVES 6 TO 8

Crunchy Chinese pea pods become the wrapper for deliciously creamy fillings, counterbalancing the crunchiness with smooth herb-flavored centers. Using fillings flavored with delicate seafood and dill, spicy curry blended with sweet chutney, or smooth Gorgonzola with crunchy pecans, these little pods will be a colorful and unusual addition to any tray of hors d'oeuvres. If you are looking for ways to cut down on the fat in this recipe, by all means use a low-fat or nonfat cream cheese and/or mayonnaise. Any leftover fillings can be spread on pita and cut into triangles for quick snacks.

PEA PODS

¹/₂ POUND FRESH CHINESE PEA PODS

Wash and trim the ends of each pea pod. Slit the top of the pea pod open.

Crab and Shrimp Filling

¹/₄ CUP MAYONNAISE

¹/₄ CUP COOKED BABY SHRIMP

¹/₄ CUP CRABMEAT

1 TEASPOON CHOPPED RED ONION

1 TABLESPOON CHOPPED FRESH DILL (OR 1 TEASPOON DRIED)

12 CLEANED PEA PODS

CHOPPED FRESH PARSLEY FOR GARNISH

In a small bowl, combine the ingredients, and refrigerate until the mixture is firm. Stuff 1 teaspoon of the mixture into each pea pod. Garnish with chopped fresh parsley.

Gorgonzola Pecan Filling

¹/₄ **CUP CRUMBLED GORGONZOLA CHEESE**

3 **OUNCES CREAM CHEESE, SOFTENED**

¹/₄ **CUP CHOPPED PECANS**

1 **TEASPOON WORCESTERSHIRE SAUCE**

12 **CLEANED PEA PODS**

Cream together the cheeses until smooth. Add the pecans and the Worcestershire sauce. Spoon the filling into the prepared pea pods. Garnish with chopped fresh parsley.

Curry and Chutney Filling

3 **OUNCES CREAM CHEESE, SOFTENED**

¹/₂ **CUP GRATED CHEDDAR CHEESE**

1 **TEASPOON SHERRY OR PORT WINE**

¹/₄ **TEASPOON CURRY POWDER**

1 **TABLESPOON MAJOR GREY'S CHUTNEY**

12 **CLEANED PEA PODS**

CHOPPED PEANUTS FOR GARNISH

Cream together the cream cheese, cheddar cheese, wine, curry, and chutney until smooth. Spread the mixture into the pea pods. Garnish with chopped peanuts.

Prosciutto Palmiers

SERVES 10 TO 12

There is nothing more elegant than an hor d'oeuvres made with puff pastry. The secret to this delectable wrap is to roll the puff pastry in grated Parmesan cheese rather than flour. This imbeds the cheese into the pastry, giving it a unique nutty flavor.

1 17¼-OUNCE PACKAGE FROZEN PUFF PASTRY SHEETS, DEFROSTED

1 CUP GRATED PARMESAN CHEESE

½ POUND PROSCIUTTO, SLICED PAPER-THIN

¼ CUP DIJON MUSTARD

Roll out each puff pastry sheet using Parmesan cheese as you would flour. Spread the pastry with Dijon mustard and cover with the prosciutto slices. Roll the puff pastry from the long side, stopping halfway. Roll the other side to the middle. Refrigerate the logs for 1 hour, for up to 2 days, or freeze for 2 months. Cut the logs into ½-inch slices. Place the slices on a cookie sheet lined with foil or parchment, and bake in a preheated oven at 400°F for 10 to 12 minutes, or until golden-brown. Serve warm.

Scraps of puff pastry can be rolled in cinnamon sugar and cut out for cookies, or rolled in grated Parmesan cheese and/or dried herbs for savory crackers. Bake at 400°F for 5 to 7 minutes, or until golden-brown.

Prosciutto-Wrapped Strawberries

SERVES 6 TO 8

Here is an example of simplicity being the height of elegance and style. Gorgeous red strawberries wrapped in slices of paper-thin prosciutto, then dipped in the tiniest bit of balsamic vinegar. On a hot summer night this is the perfect wrappetizer to serve with champagne. When strawberries are not in season, substitute orange and green melon wedges.

24 PERFECT 2-INCH STRAWBERRIES

1/2 POUND PROSCIUTTO, SLICED PAPER-THIN

3 TO 4 TABLESPOONS BALSAMIC VINEGAR

SPRIGS OF FRESH PARSLEY AND MINT FOR GARNISH

Wash the strawberries, trim the stems, and drain them on paper toweling. Cut the prosciutto slices in half. Place a slice of prosciutto on a work surface, and then roll the strawberry in the prosciutto, spearing the wrap with a toothpick. Just before serving, pour the vinegar into the serving platter, lay the strawberries on the platter, and serve, garnished with sprigs of fresh parsley and mint.

Spanakopitas

Flaky phyllo dough, encasing a colorful filling of spinach and feta cheese, makes gorgeous appetizers for any occasion. Traditional Greek Spanakopitas are made in a triangular shape, giving them just a little more personality than those wrapped as an "egg roll." These spinach rolls can be made ahead of time, then refrigerated or frozen until you are ready to serve them. Working with phyllo is easy, and the results are spectacular.

1 ONION, FINELY CHOPPED

2 TABLESPOONS OLIVE OIL

1 PACKAGE (10-OUNCE) FROZEN CHOPPED SPINACH, DEFROSTED, THEN SQUEEZED DRY

1 CUP CRUMBLED FETA CHEESE

3 EGGS

1 TEASPOON SALT

$^1/_2$ TEASPOON FRESHLY GROUND BLACK PEPPER

$^1/_8$ TEASPOON NUTMEG

$^1/_2$ POUND PHYLLO DOUGH

$^1/_2$ TO 1 CUP DRY UNFLAVORED BREAD CRUMBS

1 CUP (2 STICKS) BUTTER, MELTED THEN COOLED

In a 10-inch skillet or sauté pan, sauté the onion in the olive oil, until the onion is soft. Add the spinach, and sauté until the spinach and onions are combined, and any liquid from the spinach is absorbed. This should take about 5 minutes. Remove from pan, and place in a medium mixing bowl. Stir in the cheese, eggs, and seasonings, blending the ingredients. (You may refrigerate the filling at this point, until you are ready to use it.)

Unroll the phyllo dough on a flat work surface and cover it with a kitchen towel that is larger than the phyllo. Remove 1 sheet and brush it all over with melted butter. Sprinkle with some bread crumbs. Cut the phyllo into 3 equal parts measuring $4^1/_2$ by 6 inches. At the top of each strip, place 1 tablespoon of the spinach mixture. Beginning at the top left, fold the phyllo over the filling to form a triangle. Fold the top right over the filling, and continue to fold to the end of the strip. Brush the packet with butter, and place on a cookie sheet that has been lined with parchment or aluminum foil.

Continue to fold the appetizers until the filling is used up. Refrigerate the filled rolls for up to 2 days, or freeze for 2 months in an airtight container. When ready to serve, bake the rolls at 350°F for 15 minutes, until golden-brown. If the rolls have been frozen, cook them (frozen), adding 7 to 10 minutes to the cooking time.

To make a free-form wrap, butter 6 sheets of phyllo, stacking one on top of another. Place the filling in the center of the phyllo and bring the four corners into the center, twisting into a knot. Brush with butter and bake at 350°F for 20 to 25 minutes, until the phyllo is golden. Cut into wedges and serve.

Sushi Rolls

Okay, I know what you're thinking, I can't get this group that I live with to eat raw fish. Well, how would you feel about getting them to eat rice, vegetables, and cooked salmon, all wrapped up in a beautiful package? I am not crazy about telling people to roll raw fish, so with that in mind, I think this sushi roll will make believers out of your family. Poached salmon is laid on seasoned rice, then paired with strips of cucumber and carrot to make a beautifully patterned appetizer.

SUSHI RICE

2 CUPS SHORT-GRAIN RICE	2 TABLESPOONS SWEET SAKE OR SHERRY
2 CUPS WATER	1 TABLESPOON SUGAR
1/4 CUP RICE VINEGAR	

Place the rice and water into a 2-quart saucepan, stir, and cover the pot. Heat until the water comes to a boil. Reduce the heat to low and cook the rice for about 15 minutes. Remove rice to a mixing bowl. In a small bowl, combine the vinegar, sake, and sugar. Pour this mixture over the rice and work it in. (I find that using a fork helps to separate the rice grains.) Let the rice cool to room temperature.

SALMON

1/2 POUND SALMON FILLET	2 TEASPOONS CHOPPED FRESH DILL
1/4 CUP WHITE WINE	

Place the salmon in a microwavable dish. Pour the wine over the fish, and top with the dill. Cover with plastic wrap and microwave on High for 4 to 5 minutes. Allow to cool before proceeding.

6 SHEETS (8 INCHES) YAKI-NORI (TOASTED
DRIED SEAWEED)

1/2 POUND COOKED SALMON FILLET
(SEE ABOVE), CUT INTO 6 LONG STRIPS

2 CUPS COOKED SUSHI RICE (SEE ABOVE),
COOLED TO ROOM TEMPERATURE

2 TABLESPOONS SESAME SEEDS

1 CARROT, CUT INTO THIN STRIPS WITH A
SWIVEL PEELER

1 HOT-HOUSE CUCUMBER, CUT INTO
MATCHSTICKS

Cut a piece of foil or plastic wrap two times the size of the nori. Place the foil on a flat work surface and center the nori on the foil. Brush with a little bit of water to dampen it. Spread a generous $1/4$ to $1/3$ cup of rice on the nori, over all but the top. Place a piece of the salmon down the middle of the rice, then sprinkle with the sesame seeds. Top with the carrot and cucumber. Using the foil as a guide, wrap the sushi up tightly. When you get to the top, lightly moisten it so that the roll will stay together. Cut the Sushi Rolls into 1-inch rounds with a damp knife. Repeat with the remaining Nori. Serve with Soy Dipping Sauce (see below).

Soy Dipping Sauce

1/2 CUP SOY SAUCE

1/3 CUP RICE VINEGAR

1 TABLESPOON SUGAR

1 SCALLION (GREEN ONION), CHOPPED

1 TABLESPOON FRESHLY GRATED GINGER

1 TEASPOON SESAME OIL

1/2 TEASPOON CHILI OIL (OPTIONAL)

Bring the soy sauce, vinegar, and sugar to a boil in a small saucepan. Cool and add the remaining ingredients. Store for up to one month in the refrigerator.

Thai Spring Rolls

MAKES 4 DOZEN

Before we start, I have to warn you that Thai Spring Rolls are addictive. Crunchy, spicy, and filled with seafood and vegetables, these will be a love at first bite. But, be careful, love does not come without a price. These rolls require a bit more time than some of the others that we have made. Plan on about 2 hours to make these; from cooking the filling and letting it cool, to wrapping. You can certainly make the filling in the morning and then roll them later in the day. Also, remember that you can freeze these after you have rolled them, so you will have a ready stock at your disposal to impress all your friends. The dipping sauce is essential and, as with all Thai foods, takes a few simple ingredients and makes a highly complex flavored sauce.

$1/2$ POUND FRESH GROUND PORK

1 TABLESPOON VEGETABLE OIL

1 CUP COARSELY CHOPPED COOKED SHRIMP

$1/2$ CUP CHOPPED SHIITAKE MUSHROOMS

4 SCALLIONS (GREEN ONIONS) FINELY CHOPPED

1 CARROT, SHREDDED

$1/2$ TEASPOON SALT

1 TEASPOON SOY SAUCE

1 TEASPOON RICE WINE (MIRIN) FOUND IN ASIAN SECTION OF SUPERMARKET

1 CUP LUKEWARM WATER

12 RICE PAPER WRAPPERS, QUARTERED

4 CUPS OIL, FOR DEEP FRYING

TO GARNISH:

LETTUCE LEAVES

BUNCHES OF FRESH MINT

1 CUP SLICED CUCUMBER

BUNCHES OF FRESH CILANTRO

In a 10-inch skillet or sauté pan, cook the pork in $1/2$ tablespoon of the oil until it is no longer pink in color. Remove the pork to a colander to drain off any excess liquid. Pour the remaining tablespoon of oil into the pan, and sauté the shrimp, mushrooms, scallions, and carrot together for 1 to 2 minutes. Remove to the colander and drain. Take the contents of the colander and transfer it to a large mixing bowl, adding the salt, soy sauce, and rice wine to the meat and vegetables. Refrigerate until cool.

When the mixture is cool, place the rice paper on a flat work surface, and brush with a bit of water to make it pliable. Place 1 tablespoon of the filling near the edge of the rice paper, then fold the rice paper over the filling, fold in both sides, and roll the paper over the filling to seal. Continue to do this until all the filling is used.

In a deep fryer or sauté pan with high sides, heat the oil to 375°F. Deep-fry the rolls a few at a time, until crisp and golden-brown. Drain on paper toweling and serve on a bed of lettuce leaves garnished with fresh mint, cucumber, and cilantro.

Thai Spring Roll Dipping Sauce

$^1/_4$ CUP SUGAR

$^1/_2$ CUP WATER

$^1/_3$ CUP RICE WINE VINEGAR

$^1/_2$ TEASPOON SALT

$^1/_4$ TEASPOON CAYENNE PEPPER

$^1/_4$ CUP GRATED CARROT

$^1/_4$ CUP CHOPPED PEANUTS

In a small saucepan combine the sugar and water, bringing the mixture to a boil for 2 minutes. Remove from the heat and add the vinegar, salt, and cayenne. Refrigerate. When ready to serve, pour the dipping sauce into small individual bowls and garnish with the carrot and peanuts.

Wrapped Brie with Apricots and Dried Cranberries

SERVES 10 TO 12

Cranberries are not just for Thanksgiving anymore, now that they are sold dried in the grocery store. My favorite way to use dried cranberries is in this delectable Brie recipe. The cheese is covered with tangy apricot preserves, dried cranberries, and then wrapped in puff pasty and baked for 1 hour. The result is a creamy wheel of Brie inside a flaky puff pastry shell, flavored with the sweet tartness of apricots and cranberries. The beauty of this appetizer is that it can be prepared ahead, refrigerated for several days, or frozen for one month, then baked just before serving. Serve the Brie with baguettes and sliced raw vegetables.

2 SHEETS FROZEN PUFF PASTRY, THAWED

6-TO-8-INCH WHEEL BRIE

1 CUP APRICOT PRESERVES

2 TABLESPOONS COGNAC (OPTIONAL)

1 CUP DRIED CRANBERRIES

EGG WASH: 1 EGG BEATEN WITH 1 TABLE-SPOON WATER

FOR ACCOMPANIMENT:

BAGUETTE SLICES

CUCUMBER SLICES

CARROT SLICES

Roll out the first piece of puff pastry into a 10-inch circle. Place the Brie in the center of the puff pastry. In a small bowl, combine the preserves, cognac, and cranberries. Spread mixture over the Brie. Roll out the other puff pastry sheet into a 14-inch circle. Cover the Brie with the puff pastry. Then, using a pastry brush dipped in water, lift the sides of the bottom puff pastry, and attach them to the wheel of Brie, using the water to attach the pastry. Trim the top puff pastry circle, and crimp it to the sides, using a fork, the pastry brush, and additional water as the "glue." Cover the Brie with plastic wrap, and refrigerate for 4 hours. When ready to bake, preheat the oven to 400° F. Place the Brie on a cookie sheet that has been covered with parchment or foil. Brush the Brie with the egg wash. Bake it for 45 to 55 minutes, or until the crust is golden. Remove from the oven, and allow to sit for 20 minutes. Using the foil or parchment, slide the Brie onto a serving platter. Trim the foil or parchment so it doesn't extend beyond the Brie, surround the cheese with baguette slices, sliced cucumbers, and carrots.

Garden Patch Wraps

No more salad bowls; instead, wrap up your salad in a package and dig in! Using tortillas, lavosh, or pita, you can have your salad wrapped in unusual packages. Trying to get our families to eat healthier food is sometimes a chore, but changing the look of that healthy salad may be just what the doctor ordered. Using colorful fresh produce encased in a wrap of your choice, you may just be able to transform that meat and potatoes man of yours into a salad wrap fanatic. A portable meal, these salads could become the vehicle for your children to have picnics in the backyard without complaining that they are eating the same old sandwich or snack foods.

The keys to great salad wraps are texture, color, and flavor. Contrasting crunchy with smooth, brightly colored with more mellow shades, and spicy versus mild, your wraps will be an explosion of sensations when you bite into them. I recommend using an iceberg lettuce or cabbage for many salads, because their bland taste and crunch is just what is needed to showcase other ingredients. Rainbow-colored peppers, tomatoes, and other vegetables become the palette from which you can create gorgeous salad wraps, so feel free to substitute your favorite vegetables and flavored wrappers in any of these recipes.

Black Bean, Corn, and Salsa Wrap

Bulgur Wheat Salad Wraps

Chicken Caesar Pita

Chicken Waldorf Salad in Whole Wheat Tortillas

Chinese Chicken Salad

Cobb Salad Wraps

Egg, Dill, and Tomato Salad Wraps

Fruit and Cheese Wraps

Hot Spinach Salad Wrap

Layered Veggie Wraps

Marinated Grilled Veggie Wraps

Roast Beef and Stilton Wrap

Seafood Salad Wraps

Shrimp, Orzo, and Sun-dried Tomato Wraps

Tomato, Cucumber, and Feta Pitas

Tuna Asparagus Wraps

Black Bean, Corn, and Salsa Wrap

SERVES 6

This delicious salad is not only colorful, it is good for you. High in protein and low in fat, this rainbow of gutsy flavors should please he-man appetites and picky kids. The all-purpose salsa dressing is delicious over mixed greens, and adds zip to chicken salads as well. If you have leftover chicken or beef, feel free to add that to the salad. This salad is particularly attractive when wrapped in yellow and blue corn tortillas, but feel free to choose whichever flavor tortilla you prefer.

12 TORTILLAS (6-INCH), WARMED

2 15-OUNCE CANS BLACK BEANS, DRAINED AND RINSED

1 CUP CHOPPED JICAMA

1/4 CUP CHOPPED SCALLIONS (GREEN ONIONS)

2 CUPS CORN (EITHER FROZEN, DEFROSTED, OR FRESH CUT FROM THE COB)

1/2 CUP CHOPPED RED PEPPER

Combine all the ingredients in a 3-quart bowl. Toss with Fresh Tomato Salsa Dressing (recipe below), and refrigerate until ready to serve.

FRESH TOMATO SALSA DRESSING

2 CUPS CHOPPED FRESH TOMATOES

1/2 CUP CHOPPED AVOCADO

1/4 CUP CHOPPED RED ONION

1 CLOVE GARLIC, MINCED

1/2 CUP CHOPPED ANAHEIM CHILE PEPPER

2 TABLESPOONS CHOPPED FRESH CILANTRO

1/4 CUP FRESH LIME JUICE

3/4 CUP VEGETABLE OIL

1 TEASPOON SALT

1/4 TEASPOON FRESHLY GROUND BLACK PEPPER

In a glass bowl, whisk together the dressing ingredients. Toss with the black bean mixture.

ASSEMBLY

| TORTILLAS | SOUR CREAM FOR GARNISH (OPTIONAL) |
| BLACK BEAN AND SALSA MIXTURE | |

Place 2 tortillas on a serving plate. Using a slotted spoon, fill each with $^1/_2$ cup black bean mixture. Fold over and serve. Garnish with sour cream, if desired.

> To store salad greens, wash and spin dry in a salad spinner. Store the greens in vegetable storage bags (they are punctured with holes), or in an airtight storage bag with one paper towel to help absorb extra moisture. Your greens should keep for up to 7 days when stored in this manner.

Bulgur Wheat Salad Wraps

SERVES 6

Tabbouleh, a cracked wheat salad with origins in the Middle East, is delicious wrapped in whole lettuce leaves and served with grilled lamb, steak, or chicken. Fresh mint, parsley, and vine-ripened tomatoes make this a cool and unusual side dish.

$1/2$ CUP BULGUR (CRACKED WHEAT)

$1/2$ CUP FINELY CHOPPED SCALLIONS (GREEN ONIONS)

1 CUP MINCED FRESH PARSLEY

$1/2$ CUP CHOPPED FRESH MINT

2 CUPS CHOPPED FRESH TOMATOES

$1/3$ CUP LEMON JUICE

$1/2$ TEASPOON SALT

$1/4$ TEASPOON BLACK PEPPER

$1/3$ CUP OLIVE OIL

10 RED LEAF LETTUCE LEAVES

Soak the bulgur in cold water for 15 minutes. Drain, and squeeze as much moisture out of it as you can. Place the bulgur in a large mixing bowl. Add the scallions, parsley, mint, and chopped tomatoes. Pour the lemon juice over the mixture and toss with the salt and pepper. Taste the mixture for seasoning, adjust if necessary. Add the oil, stirring to combine. Place $1/3$ cup of the mixture in the center of a lettuce leaf. Fold the lettuce over the salad, and place seam-side down on a salad plate, garnished with additional chopped parsley and mint. Repeat until all wraps are completed.

Chicken Caesar Pita

SERVES 6 TO 8

*One of my all-time favorites is a chicken Caesar salad. There is
something delightful about the pairing of warm grilled chicken
and cool romaine lettuce, then tossing it with a creamy garlic-
scented dressing. Wrapping this in a pita makes a terrific lunch
or dinner for your family. The Caesar dressing will keep in the
refrigerator for 5 days, and feel free to use leftover chicken or
shrimp rather than grilling chicken for this wrap.*

6 TO 8 PITAS (12-INCH)

CHICKEN

3 WHOLE CHICKEN BREASTS, BONED AND
SKINNED

$1/2$ CUP SOY SAUCE

1 TEASPOON GRATED GINGER

$1/4$ CUP VEGETABLE OIL

$1/4$ CUP RICE WINE (MIRIN), OR DRY
SHERRY

1 TEASPOON MINCED GARLIC

Combine the oil, soy sauce, rice wine, ginger, and garlic in a zipper-type storage bag.
Marinate the chicken in this mixture for 2 hours. Preheat a charcoal grill or broiler.
Drain the chicken from the marinade and grill 4 inches from the heat source for 3 to 4
minutes on each side, or until the chicken is no longer pink in the middle. After cooking the chicken, cut it diagonally into 8 to 10 strips.

CAESAR SALAD

1 EGG

1 TABLESPOON WORCESTERSHIRE SAUCE

1 CLOVE CRUSHED GARLIC

$1/2$ TO $3/4$ CUP VEGETABLE OIL

2 TO 3 TABLESPOONS FRESH LEMON JUICE

$1/2$ TEASPOON SALT (OPTIONAL)

$1/4$ TEASPOON FRESHLY GROUND BLACK
PEPPER

8 CUPS TORN ROMAINE LETTUCE (3 LARGE
HEADS)

1 CUP FRESHLY GRATED PARMESAN CHEESE

In a small glass mixing bowl, or in the bowl of a food processor, blend the egg, Worcestershire sauce, oil, lemon juice, and salt and pepper. Taste the dressing for seasoning, and add additional lemon juice, Worcestershire, or salt and pepper if desired.

Place the lettuce in a large salad bowl. Toss the salad with the dressing, adding the cheese as you go.

ASSEMBLY

PITA BREADS	COOKED CHICKEN
CAESAR SALAD	LEMON WEDGES FOR GARNISH

To assemble each wrap, place the pita on a work surface or cutting board. Spoon 1 cup salad onto the center of the pita, and top with four or five slices of cooked chicken. Beginning at the bottom, roll up the pita and secure the sandwich in two places with a toothpick. Cut each wrap in half and serve garnished with lemon wedges.

Chicken Waldorf Salad in Whole Wheat Tortillas

SERVES 6

Traditional Waldorf salad gets a makeover with the addition of chicken, then it's wrapped in whole wheat tortillas. If you would like to cut down on the amount of fat in this recipe, feel free to use a low-fat or nonfat variety of mayonnaise.

3 CUPS DICED COOKED CHICKEN

1 CUP CHOPPED APPLE (I LIKE TO USE A FIRM, SWEET APPLE, SUCH AS A GALA)

1 CUP CHOPPED CELERY

$^1/_2$ CUP GOLDEN RAISINS

$^1/_2$ CUP CHOPPED WALNUTS

1 TABLESPOON CHOPPED FRESH PARSLEY

$^1/_2$ CUP MAYONNAISE

1 TABLESPOON LEMON JUICE

12 WHOLE WHEAT TORTILLAS (6-INCH)

$^1/_2$ CUP APPLE WEDGES FOR GARNISH

$^1/_2$ CUP CHOPPED FRESH PARSLEY FOR GARNISH

Combine the chicken, apple, celery, raisins, walnuts, and parsley in a salad bowl. In a small glass mixing bowl, blend the mayonnaise and the lemon juice. Pour the dressing over the salad, then toss to coat. Refrigerate until ready to serve. Place $^1/_2$ cup salad in the center of the first tortilla. Starting at the bottom, fold the bottom of the tortilla toward the center. Fold the top and sides in the same manner to make a letter-like package. Continue until all tortillas are wrapped. Place on individual plates, allowing 2 tortillas per person. Garnish the tortillas with apple wedges and fresh parsley.

Chinese Chicken Salad

SERVES 6

One of my favorite salads is a Chinese-inspired chicken salad. There are so many variations, some using a light, sesame-based dressing, others a soy dressing, and still others a Hoisin sauce dressing. My personal favorite is wrapped in a flour tortilla, bursting with crunchy vegetables and chicken in a deliciously light, sweet, and pungent dressing. Serve the salad in warm tortillas, making the coolness of the salad a wonderful complement to the warm tortilla.

3 CUPS SHREDDED COOKED CHICKEN

4 SCALLIONS (GREEN ONIONS), CHOPPED

1 RED BELL PEPPER, CUT INTO JULIENNE STRIPS

8 CUPS MIXED TORN LETTUCE LEAVES (SUCH AS ROMAINE, RED LEAF, AND BOSTON)

1 CUP SNOW PEAS, TRIMMED, AND MICROWAVED ON HIGH FOR 1 MINUTE

1 CUP COARSELY GRATED CARROT

$^{1}/_{2}$ CUP DRY-ROASTED CASHEWS

12 FLOUR TORTILLAS (6-INCH), WARMED

Combine all the ingredients, except the tortillas, in a large salad bowl.

GINGER SOY DRESSING

$^{1}/_{4}$ CUP SOY SAUCE

$^{1}/_{2}$ CUP RICE WINE VINEGAR

$^{3}/_{4}$ CUP VEGETABLE OIL

$^{1}/_{3}$ CUP SUGAR

2 TABLESPOONS SESAME OIL

$^{1}/_{4}$ CUP SESAME SEEDS

1 TABLESPOON GRATED GINGERROOT

In a glass bowl, whisk together all the dressing ingredients until emulsified. Store in the refrigerator for up to 2 weeks. Remove dressing from the refrigerator and shake well to blend.

ASSEMBLY

CHICKEN SALAD

GINGER SOY DRESSING

TORTILLAS

CHOPPED FRESH CILANTRO FOR GARNISH
(OPTIONAL)

When ready to serve, toss the salad with the dressing. Place ¹/₂ cup salad into each warm tortilla, filling as you would a taco. Serve 2 per person. Garnish with chopped fresh cilantro, if desired.

To warm tortillas

In the microwave: Stack 6 tortillas on a plate lined with paper toweling. Cover the stack with another paper towel and microwave on high for 1¹/₂ to 2 minutes. Remove from the microwave and serve.

In the oven: Arrange 10 tortillas on aluminum foil and seal the foil. Place the tortillas on a cookie sheet and bake in a preheated 350°F oven for 15 to 20 minutes. Remove from the oven and serve.

Cobb Salad Wraps

SERVES 6 TO 8

Cobb Salad is standard fare on menus in California. Served to movie stars at the famed Brown Derby Restaurant, it became the salad that defined the golden years in Hollywood. Today, you can enjoy this reminder of days gone by, tucked into a pita, for lunch or dinner. Make sure to garnish the plates with additional chopped veggies and finely chopped hard-cooked eggs.

1 CUP CHOPPED ICEBERG LETTUCE

1 CUP CHOPPED ROMAINE LETTUCE

2 TABLESPOONS CHOPPED CHIVES

2 MEDIUM-SIZED VINE-RIPENED TOMATOES, DICED

1 WHOLE CHICKEN BREAST, COOKED, BONED, SKINNED, AND DICED

6 STRIPS BACON, COOKED AND CRUMBLED

1 HAAS AVOCADO, PEELED AND DICED

3 HARD-COOKED EGGS, DICED

$1/2$ CUP CRUMBLED BLUE CHEESE

$1/4$ CUP RED WINE VINEGAR

$1/2$ TEASPOON SUGAR

1 TABLESPOON LEMON JUICE

$1/2$ TEASPOON SALT

1 TEASPOON WORCESTERSHIRE SAUCE

$1/2$ TEASPOON DRY MUSTARD

1 CLOVE GARLIC, MINCED

1 CUP VEGETABLE OIL

6 PITAS (6-INCH)

Place the lettuces, chives, tomatoes, chicken, bacon, avocado, hard-cooked eggs, and blue cheese in a large salad bowl. In a mixing bowl, combine the vinegar, sugar, lemon juice, salt, Worcestershire, mustard, garlic, and oil, whisking to blend. Pour the dressing over the salad, and toss until the salad is coated. Split a pita in half, and stuff each pocket with $1/2$ to $3/4$ cup of the salad mixture. Repeat until all pitas are stuffed. Garnish and serve.

Egg, Dill, and Tomato Salad Wraps

SERVES 6

Eggs have gotten a lot of bad press in the past few years. This egg salad with additional whites not only cuts down on the amount of yolks used to produce a delicious salad, but also does so without all the cholesterol. The delicate flavor of dill is a perfect pairing with the egg salad, which is then stuffed into whole tomatoes that have been hollowed out. This is a wonderful spring luncheon dish.

10 HARD-COOKED EGGS (SEE BELOW)

2 TABLESPOONS CHOPPED FRESH DILL

1 TEASPOON CHOPPED FRESH CHIVES

1/2 CUP CHOPPED CELERY

1/2 CUP MAYONNAISE

1 TEASPOON DIJON MUSTARD

6 LARGE VINE-RIPENED TOMATOES

ADDITIONAL CHOPPED FRESH DILL FOR GARNISH

In a mixing bowl, mash 10 of the egg whites and 4 of the egg yolks, saving the other yolks for another use. Blend in the dill, chives, celery, mayonnaise, and mustard until well combined. Refrigerate until ready to serve.

Remove the tops from each tomato, and, using a grapefruit knife or other small knife, also remove the meat of the tomato, preserving the shell. Turn the tomatoes upside down and drain on paper toweling. When ready to serve, stuff the tomatoes with the egg mixture, and garnish with additional chopped dill.

Perfectly Hard-cooked Eggs

Lay the eggs in a pan of water and add water to cover by 1 inch. Bring the water to a boil and turn the heat off. Let the eggs sit in the water for 15 minutes. At the end of 15 minutes, plunge the eggs into a bowl filled with water and ice. This helps to prevent the dark line that forms between the yolk and the white. Allow the eggs to sit in the water 10 to 15 minutes, then peel under running water. Chill the eggs after peeling until ready to use.

Fruit and Cheese Wraps

SERVES 4

Amazing that anything so delectable could be so simple to make. These wraps are ready in under 15 minutes, and make a superb lunch or light dinner. Whether you serve these in pita halves, or lettuce leaves, they make a wonderful addition to your repertoire.

1 1/2 CUPS PECAN HALVES

2 TABLESPOONS BALSAMIC VINEGAR

1 TEASPOON DIJON MUSTARD

1/2 TEASPOON SALT

DASH OF FRESHLY GROUND PEPPER

1/2 TEASPOON SUGAR

1/4 CUP VEGETABLE OIL

2 PEARS (RED PEARS ARE BEST)

2 MEDIUM-SIZE GRANNY SMITH APPLES

1 TABLESPOON FRESH LEMON JUICE

2 CUPS SEEDLESS RED GRAPES, CUT IN HALF LENGTHWISE

1/2 POUND GRUYÈRE CHEESE, CUT INTO MATCHSTICKS

4 PITAS, OR 8 LETTUCE LEAVES (WASHED AND DRAINED)

CHOPPED FRESH PARSLEY AND PECAN HALVES FOR GARNISH

Preheat the oven to 350°F, and toast the pecans on a baking sheet for about 8 minutes, or until they are fragrant. Be careful not to burn them. Cool the pecans, then chop coarsely. In a small bowl, whisk together the vinegar and mustard. Add the salt, pepper, sugar, and oil, whisking until smooth. Core the pears and apples, cut them into 1/2-inch dice. Place them in a bowl and toss them with the lemon juice. Add the grapes and Gruyère, and toss with the dressing. Add the pecans, and toss again. Halve the pitas and stuff each pocket with 1/2 cup salad. Serve garnished with chopped fresh parsley and additional pecans.

If you would rather serve this salad in fresh lettuce, place 1/2 cup of salad in the middle of each lettuce leaf, then fold the lettuce over the filling and secure with a toothpick, if desired.

Hot Spinach Salad Wrap

SERVES 6

Covered with a warm sweet-and-sour dressing made from bacon and Dijon mustard, serve this delicious wrap as the salad course at dinner, or a main course at lunch. Fresh baby spinach is now available bagged in the produce section of your grocery, so there is no excuse not to eat your spinach!

2 BAGS (10-OUNCE) BABY SPINACH

2 HARD-COOKED EGGS, CHOPPED

5 STRIPS BACON, CUT INTO 1-INCH DICE (SUBSTITUTE TURKEY BACON IF YOU PREFER)

1/2 CUP CHOPPED RED ONION

2 TABLESPOONS DIJON MUSTARD

1/2 CUP BROWN SUGAR

1/4 CUP RICE WINE VINEGAR

6 PITAS (6-INCH)

Place the spinach and eggs in a large salad bowl. In a 10-inch skillet, cook the bacon until crisp. Add the onion, and sauté until it is translucent. Add the mustard and brown sugar, stirring until the sugar melts and the dressing bubbles. Add the vinegar and allow some of it to burn off, about 1 minute. Pour the dressing over the spinach and toss. Halve the pitas and fill each pocket with salad mixture. Serve warm.

Layered Veggie Wraps

A layered vegetarian salad featuring lavosh, bursting with fresh veggies, and using homemade ranch-style salad dressing, this wrap will have your family clamoring for more. Feel free to vary the vegetables during the seasons, to add texture and crunch to this delicious rolled salad. Another variation is to finely chop all the veggies and layer as directed. The result is a pinwheel kaleidoscope wrap!

$^1/_2$ CUP SOUR CREAM

1 CUP MAYONNAISE

$^1/_2$ CUP MILK

2 TABLESPOONS FRESH DILL (1 TABLESPOON DRIED)

1 TEASPOON GRATED LEMON ZEST

2 CHOPPED SCALLIONS (GREEN ONIONS)

$^1/_4$ CUP CHOPPED FRESH PARSLEY

$^1/_2$ TEASPOON DRIED OREGANO

$^1/_4$ TEASPOON DRIED TARRAGON

$^1/_4$ TEASPOON GROUND BLACK PEPPER

10 RED LEAF LETTUCE LEAVES, WASHED AND DRIED

2 ROMA TOMATOES, THINLY SLICED

1 MEDIUM RED ONION, THINLY SLICED

2 SMALL ZUCCHINI, THINLY SLICED, LENGTHWISE

2 CARROTS, COARSELY GRATED

1 HAAS AVOCADO, THINLY SLICED AND SPRINKLED WITH LIME OR LEMON JUICE TO PRESERVE COLOR

1 CUP FRESH ALFALFA SPROUTS

2 SHEETS LAVOSH

In a small bowl, blend together the sour cream, mayonnaise, milk, and seasonings, whisking until smooth. Refrigerate for up to 2 weeks. Lay 1 sheet of lavosh on a work surface or cutting board, and spread a thin layer of dressing over it. Lay the lettuce leaves over the dressing layer, and then half of the vegetables. Roll up the lavosh from the short side. Repeat with the remaining sheet of lavosh. Wrap in plastic wrap or foil for 1 to 2 hours. Slice the rolls into 2-inch rounds, and serve 2 per person.

Lemons make a great alternative to vinegar in salad dressings. Try them for a sunny new flavor.

Marinated Grilled Veggie Wraps

SERVES 6

Which wrap is your favorite? Everyone has asked that question, and without a doubt it is this wrap. It's filled with grilled vegetables that have been marinated in balsamic vinegar and fresh herbs. Prepared almost like a terrine, the vegetables are layered, then refrigerated before serving. The pita is spread with goat cheese, and then slices of the terrine are placed into the pockets. To simplify the grilling, we will be broiling the vegetables. If you would like to use your charcoal grill, feel free to do so; it gives the dish a wonderful smoky flavor. The trick for this dish is to have all the vegetables sliced the same thickness, so that they cook uniformly.

1 PURPLE EGGPLANT, SLICED INTO $^1/_2$-INCH SLICES

1 GREEN PEPPER, SLICED INTO $^1/_2$-INCH SLICES

1 RED PEPPER, SLICED INTO $^1/_2$-INCH SLICES

1 YELLOW PEPPER, SLICED INTO $^1/_2$-INCH SLICES

2 RED ONIONS, SLICED INTO $^1/_2$-INCH ROUNDS

2 ZUCCHINI, SLICED LENGTHWISE INTO $^1/_2$-INCH SLICES

2 YELLOW SQUASH, SLICED LENGTHWISE INTO $^1/_2$-INCH SLICES

SALT AND FRESHLY GROUND PEPPER, TO SEASON

OLIVE OIL FOR BRUSHING VEGETABLES

SALT TO TASTE

FRESHLY GROUND BLACK PEPPER TO TASTE

$^1/_2$ CUP BALSAMIC VINEGAR

$^1/_4$ CUP OLIVE OIL

$^1/_4$ CUP VEGETABLE OIL

3 CLOVES GARLIC, MASHED

$^1/_4$ CUP CHOPPED FRESH BASIL

2 TABLESPOONS CHOPPED FRESH PARSLEY

$^1/_2$ CUP GOAT CHEESE

6 PITAS

Arrange the vegetables on a jelly-roll pan that has been fitted with a sheet of aluminum foil. Brush the vegetables with a little of the olive oil and season with salt and pepper. Preheat the broiler for 10 minutes. Broil 4 inches from the heat source, until the vegetables become soft. Turn the vegetables and broil for another 5 to 7 minutes. Remove from broiler and set them aside while you prepare the marinade. In a small glass mixing bowl, combine the vinegar, oils, garlic, and herbs, whisking the mixture together. Using a 9 × 13-inch pan, layer the vegetables, beginning with the eggplant. After each layer is completed, spoon on about 2 tablespoons of the marinade. When finished layering, spoon the remaining marinade over the vegetables. Cover with plastic wrap and refrigerate for 4 hours or overnight. When you are ready to serve, halve the pitas open, and spread insides with a thin layer of goat cheese. Slice a portion of the layered vegetables and stuff it into each pita pocket. Makes a great "side" with Chicken and Red Potato Wraps.

Roast Beef and Stilton Wrap

SERVES 6 TO 8

Leftover roast beef never seems to taste as good the next day. This salad will change your mind about recycled roast beef. When tossed together with snow peas, carrots, red pepper, and tangy Stilton cheese, this wrap may taste even better than last night's dinner. Make sure to trim the beef of all its fat, and slice it thinly. It is best to have all the components ready to wrap just before serving. I like to use Boston or Bibb lettuce to wrap these salads.

1 TABLESPOON SESAME OIL

1 TABLESPOON VEGETABLE OIL

2 CUPS LEFTOVER COOKED ROAST BEEF, TRIMMED OF FAT, AND SLICED THINLY OR JULIENNED

2 MEDIUM CARROTS, CUT INTO MATCH-STICKS

1 CUP SNOW PEAS, TRIMMED, AND CUT ON THE DIAGONAL

1 RED PEPPER, THINLY SLICED

1/3 CUP STILTON CHEESE

1/3 CUP MAYONNAISE

1/4 CUP SOUR CREAM

1 TABLESPOON RICE VINEGAR

4 DASHES TABASCO

FRESHLY GROUND BLACK PEPPER TO TASTE

1 TABLESPOON WORCESTERSHIRE SAUCE

8 WHOLE LETTUCE LEAVES, CLEANED AND DRIED

MIXED GREENS FOR PRESENTATION

GRATED CARROT FOR GARNISH

RED PEPPER SLICES FOR GARNISH

In a wok or large sauté pan, heat the oils over medium-high heat, add the beef and vegetables, tossing to coat with the oil until heated through. Transfer to a large mixing bowl. In another small bowl, mash the Stilton cheese, and gradually blend in the mayonnaise, sour cream, rice vinegar, Tabasco, pepper, and Worcestershire sauce. Refrigerate dressing until ready to serve.

Toss the salad with the dressing, and place 1/2 to 3/4 cup of it in the center of each lettuce leaf. Fold the bottom of the lettuce leaf over the filling, fold in the sides, and then roll the lettuce over the filling. Secure with a toothpick if necessary. Serve on a bed of mixed greens, surrounded by additional grated carrot and red pepper slices.

Seafood Salad Wraps

*In New England an example of simple culinary magic is the tradi-
tional lobster roll. Chunks of Maine lobster mixed with the tiniest
bit of mayonnaise and finely diced celery are stuffed into a grilled
hotdog bun with the sides shaved off. The result is a taste of heav-
en on earth. My salute to this fabulous wrap is the Seafood Salad
Wrap—chunks of shrimp, crab, and lobster wrapped in lavosh,
bursting with a fresh taste that doesn't overpower the delicate
shellfish. You can serve this for a special occasion, or surprise
your family and treat them to this on the spur of the moment.*

2 CUPS CHOPPED COOKED MEDIUM SHRIMP	2 TABLESPOONS KETCHUP
1 CUP CRABMEAT	1/2 TEASPOON DRIED TARRAGON, OR 2 TEASPOONS FRESH
2 CUPS CHOPPED COOKED LOBSTER MEAT	1 TEASPOON WORCESTERSHIRE SAUCE
1/2 CUP FINELY CHOPPED CELERY	1 TEASPOON PREPARED HORSERADISH
2 TABLESPOONS CHOPPED FRESH PARSLEY	2 SHEETS LAVOSH
1 CUP MAYONNAISE	CHOPPED FRESH PARSLEY FOR GARNISH

Combine the seafood with the celery in a large mixing bowl. In a smaller bowl, combine the parsley, mayonnaise, ketchup, tarragon, Worcestershire, and horseradish.
Pour the dressing over the seafood and stir to blend. Lay the lavosh on a flat surface,
and spread half of the seafood mixture over it. Roll, then repeat with the remaining
lavosh. Wrap rolls in plastic wrap and refrigerate for 1 hour, or overnight. When ready
to serve, cut the lavosh into 2-inch pieces. Serve garnished with chopped fresh parsley.

Shrimp, Orzo, and Sun-dried Tomato Wraps

SERVES 8

A gorgeous jumble of color and texture packed into lavosh, this salad will become a favorite all year long. Feel free to substitute chicken for the shrimp, and to add more garlic and sun-dried tomatoes to suit your taste. Orzo is rice-shaped pasta; it's sold in the dry pasta section of the grocery store.

3 CUPS WATER

1 CUP ORZO

$^1/_2$ TEASPOON SALT

$^1/_3$ CUP VEGETABLE OIL

$^1/_3$ CUP RED WINE VINEGAR

SALT AND FRESHLY GROUND PEPPER, TO TASTE

2 TABLESPOONS FINELY MINCED GARLIC

$^1/_2$ CUP CHOPPED SUN-DRIED TOMATOES, PACKED IN OIL, DRAINED

$^1/_3$ CUP OLIVE OIL

$^1/_2$ CUP FINELY CHOPPED RED ONION

$^1/_4$ CUP CHOPPED FLAT-LEAF PARSLEY

$^1/_3$ CUP CHOPPED FRESH BASIL

1 POUND COOKED MEDIUM SHRIMP, PEELED AND DEVEINED

2 SHEETS LAVOSH

ADDITIONAL CHOPPED PARSLEY AND BASIL FOR GARNISH

Bring the water to a boil over high heat. Add the orzo and $^1/_2$ teaspoon salt, bringing the water to a boil again. Reduce the heat and simmer for 15 minutes. Drain the pasta. In a small bowl, combine the vegetable oil, vinegar, and salt and pepper to taste. Toss the pasta with the mixture, and allow the orzo to come to room temperature. In a small sauté pan, heat the garlic and sun-dried tomatoes in the olive oil. Add the shrimp and onions, just to coat them. Combine with the orzo, then fold in the parsley and basil. Taste for salt and pepper, and correct if necessary. Chill.

Place the lavosh on a cutting board and cut it into 4 equal parts. (You should have 4 8-inch squares.) Place $^1/_2$ to $^3/_4$ cup of the salad in the center of the first square. Fold the lower portion of the lavosh up over the salad. Fold in the sides, and lastly, roll the lavosh over to the top. Continue until you complete all 4 lavosh squares. Cut each in half and serve garnished with additional parsley and basil.

Tomato, Cucumber, and Feta Pitas

SERVES 4 TO 6

Cool and refreshing, this vegetarian wrap can be served as an accompaniment for grilled steak or fish, or as a luncheon course. The salad can be made a day ahead of time, and then wrapped just before serving. To add more spice to the salad, try one of the new flavored feta cheeses, one with basil and sun-dried tomato or peppercorns.

2 LARGE, VINE-RIPENED TOMATOES, CHOPPED (ABOUT 2 CUPS)

1 CUP CHOPPED CUCUMBER

1/2 CUP CHOPPED RED ONION

1 CUP PITTED KALAMATA OLIVES

3/4 CUP VEGETABLE OIL

1/3 CUP WHITE VINEGAR

2 TEASPOONS SUGAR

2 TABLESPOONS DRIED DILLWEED

1 CLOVE GARLIC, MINCED

1 TEASPOON DRIED OREGANO

1/2 TEASPOON FRESHLY GROUND BLACK PEPPER

1/2 CUP CRUMBLED FETA CHEESE

6 PITAS (6-INCH)

CHOPPED FRESH DILL FOR GARNISH

In a large glass bowl, combine the tomato, cucumber, red onion, and olives. In another bowl, whisk together the oil, vinegar, sugar, spices, and feta. Pour this over the tomato mixture and toss. Refrigerate for at least 1 hour. When ready to serve, cut the pitas in half and fill each pocket with salad. Garnish with chopped fresh dill. Kabob wraps are a wonderful companion to this recipe.

Tuna Asparagus Wraps

SERVES 6

This wrap combines the delicate flavor of dill with tuna salad and asparagus complimented by zesty lemon pepper, giving you a salad wrap that becomes a rolled mosaic when served. I like to use pencil-thin asparagus in this wrap, and fresh dill to flavor and garnish the plate. It transforms ordinary tuna salad into an extraordinary luncheon dish.

$^1/_2$ POUND ASPARAGUS

2 CANS (6-OUNCE) ALBACORE TUNA, DRAINED

$^1/_2$ CUP CHOPPED CELERY

1 TABLESPOON CHOPPED ONION

$^1/_4$ CUP CHOPPED RED PEPPER

2 TABLESPOONS CHOPPED FRESH DILL

$^3/_4$ CUP MAYONNAISE

1 TEASPOON LEMON PEPPER

2 SHEETS LAVOSH

Trim the asparagus, then cut into uniform lengths. Arrange the asparagus in a steamer basket, and place over boiling water, steaming until the asparagus is crisp but tender, about 4 minutes depending upon the thickness of the asparagus. Remove, drain, and chill.

In a mixing bowl, combine the tuna, celery, onion, red pepper, chopped dill, mayonnaise, and lemon pepper, stirring to blend. Lay the lavosh on a flat surface or cutting board. Spread a thin layer of the tuna salad over the first lavosh, covering it. Lay the asparagus across the lavosh, leaving 1-inch spaces between each. Roll the lavosh, then wrap in plastic wrap until ready to serve. Repeat with the remaining lavosh. Cut each into 2-inch slices and serve. Garnish the plate with additional chopped fresh dill.

Meals Under Wraps

Meals under wraps are an idea whose time has come. It's time to make the blue plate into a fashion plate. A flat plate is boring. By rolling your food, you not only give the plate pizzazz, but cut into that rolled wrap and you will find a mosaic of taste and texture you never imagined. Fusion in the kitchen awaits when you begin to use edible wraps for your meals. Blending cuisines from around the world, you will be able to excite the palate and warm the hearts of those you love. What the casserole did for home cooks in the fifties, wraps will do for you in the nineties. And, incorporating all the ingredients into a wrapper instead of a casserole dish not only makes a nutritious meal, but also a food fashion statement.

By wrapping some of your old favorites we'll create new eating adventures. Using edible wrappers is also a way to try new cuisines and tastes. Rather than serving a chicken casserole, spice up that chicken; keep it under wraps, and serve Coco Loco Chicken Quesadillas. Ordinary grilled fish takes on a new look, and flavor, when rolled with salsa and cabbage salad in corn tortillas, producing Grilled Fish Tacos Especial.

By wrapping up leftovers, you can recycle Tuesday's chicken into Curried Chicken and Shrimp Wraps or Barbecue Chicken Wraps. Just as everyday meals benefit from being wrapped, special-occasion dinners take on new elegance when they are wrapped. Whether you serve filet mignon and garlic mashed potatoes wrapped in delicate phyllo, or creamy Seafood Lasagna Wraps, dinner for the boss will never be the same again. Whatever meal it is, wrap it up!

Artichoke Soufflé Wrap

Barbecue Chicken Wraps

Beijing City Chicken Wrapped in Lettuce Leaves

Blackened Snapper Wraps

Breakfast Strudels

Broccoli, Mushroom, and Cheese Calzone

Carne Asada Fajitas

Chicken and Red Potato Wraps

Chicken Parmesan Wraps

Coco Loco Quesadilla Wraps

Confetti Philly Steak Wraps

Covent Garden Market Wraps

Curried Chicken and Shrimp Wraps

Eggplant Wraps

Falafel Wraps

Grilled Fish Tacos Especial

Kebab Wraps

Korean Beef Rolls

Mango Snapper Wraps

Omelette Wraps

Peking Duck Wraps

Pesto Swordfish Wraps

Pilgrim Dinner Wraps

Pizza Wraps

Quesadilla Mercedes

Ratatouille Crêpes

Roti

Rocky Balboa Calzone

Salmon Pitas

Sausage and Pepper Wraps

Seafood Lasagna Wraps

Sesame Chicken Wraps

Sole Wraps

Spicy Shrimp and Black Bean Wraps

Steak and Garlic Mashed Potato Wraps

Stuffed Cabbage Rolls

Tandoori Chicken Wraps

Teriyaki Chicken Wraps

Thai Shrimp and Peanut Sauce Wraps

Artichoke Soufflé Wrap

SERVES 6 TO 8

The classic French-rolled soufflé gets a makeover when it is jazzed up with artichokes, then wrapped around shrimp flavored with dill and Gruyère cheese. This makes a winning combination in an elegant lunch, brunch, or dinner entrée. This soufflé is easily put together, and each step can be made ahead of time, or you can bake and freeze the soufflé for up to one month before serving. Don't let the word soufflé scare you from trying this easy dish. The worry is taken out of this since it is only one inch high. You cannot ruin it, I promise!

NON-STICK COOKING SPRAY

3 TABLESPOONS BUTTER

$^1/_2$ CUP FINELY CHOPPED ONION

3 TABLESPOONS ALL-PURPOSE FLOUR

2 CUPS MILK

$^1/_2$ TEASPOON SALT

6 EGG YOLKS

1 CAN (15-OUNCE) ARTICHOKE HEARTS, DRAINED AND CHOPPED

6 EGG WHITES

1 POUND MEDIUM SHRIMP, PEELED, DEVEINED, AND COOKED

1 CUP GRATED GRUYÈRE CHEESE

2 TABLESPOONS CHOPPED FRESH DILL

ADDITIONAL SHRIMP AND ARTICHOKE HEARTS FOR GARNISH

LEMON WEDGES FOR GARNISH

SPRIGS OF FRESH DILL FOR GARNISH

Preheat the oven to 400°F. Line a 10 × 15-inch jelly roll pan with aluminum foil, extending the foil 2 inches over the pan at each end. Press the foil into the pan and spray with nonstick cooking spray.

Melt the butter in a 3-quart saucepan. Add the onion and continue cooking over low heat. Stir in the flour, and whisk until it begins to bubble. Add the milk, whisking constantly over medium-high heat, until the sauce comes to a boil. Turn off heat and remove 1 cup of sauce to a bowl, adding the egg yolks and artichoke hearts. Set the remaining sauce aside. In the large bowl of an electric mixer, beat the egg whites until stiff. Stir into the artichoke heart mixture. Spread into the prepared pan and bake for 15 minutes, or until the top is golden and a toothpick inserted into the soufflé comes out clean. While the soufflé is cooking, make the filling. Dice the shrimp, and add it with the cheese and dill to the reserved sauce. When the soufflé comes out of the oven, have a sheet of foil cut that is 4 inches longer than the jelly-roll pan. Place the foil over the soufflé and in one motion turn the soufflé out onto a flat surface with the foil on the bottom. Remove the baking foil, being careful not to cut into the soufflé. Spread the soufflé with the sauce, then gently roll from the short end, using the foil to help you. If you would like to store the soufflé roll, wrap it in the foil and refrigerate for up to 2 days, or freeze for up to 2 weeks. Defrost, in the refrigerator, and bake in a 400°F oven for 20 to 30 minutes, or until heated through. If you are serving the soufflé immediately, use two large spatulas to remove it to a serving platter, garnish with additional shrimp and artichoke hearts, lemon wedges, and sprigs of fresh dill. Slice into 3/4-to-1-inch slices.

Barbecue Chicken Wraps

A takeoff on that wonderful invention, the designer pizza, this wrap uses pita wrapped around barbecued chicken, smoked Gouda, cilantro, and red onions. Life doesn't get much better than this.

6 PITAS (6-INCH)

2 CUPS WESTERN BARBECUE SAUCE (SEE RECIPE, PAGE 82)

2 CUPS CHOPPED COOKED CHICKEN

$1/2$ POUND SMOKED GOUDA CHEESE, CUT INTO $1/4$-INCH SLICES

$1/2$ MEDIUM RED ONION, SLICED THINLY

$1/4$ CUP CHOPPED CILANTRO

ADDITIONAL BARBECUE SAUCE AND CHOPPED CILANTRO FOR GARNISH

Preheat the oven to 400°F. Set the pitas on a cookie sheet. Spread each with $1/4$ cup Western Barbecue Sauce. Top with chicken, smoked Gouda, and onion. Bake the pitas for 15 to 20 minutes, until the cheese is melted and golden-brown. Remove from the oven, sprinkle the top with chopped cilantro, and roll up. Secure with toothpicks. Serve with additional barbecue sauce and chopped cilantro.

Western Barbecue Sauce

MAKES ABOUT 3 CUPS

Easy and delicious, you may want to get rid of that store-bought barbecue sauce in your fridge. This will keep for 1 month in the refrigerator.

2 TABLESPOONS BUTTER

1/2 CUP CHOPPED ONION

2 GARLIC CLOVES, MINCED

2 CUPS TOMATO PUREE

1/4 CUP RED WINE VINEGAR

1 TEASPOON TABASCO SAUCE

2 TABLESPOONS WORCESTERSHIRE SAUCE

1 CUP BROWN SUGAR

1/2 CUP APPLE JUICE

Melt the butter in a small saucepan, then add the onion and garlic. Sauté for 2 or 3 minutes, until the vegetables have released their oils. Add the remaining ingredients and bring to a simmer. Cook for 15 to 20 minutes. Taste for seasoning and adjust if necessary. If you prefer your sauce sweeter, add additional brown sugar; if you prefer it hotter, add more Tabasco. Refrigerate until ready to use.

Beijing City Chicken Wrapped in Lettuce Leaves

SERVES 6

A takeoff on a dish served at the Beijing City Restaurant in Hong Kong, this quick chicken dish is flavored with Hoisin sauce and wrapped in lettuce leaves, for a low-fat entree. The chicken can be prepared a day ahead of time, and stir-fried right before serving. Wash the lettuce leaves the day before, dry well, and store in the refrigerator. Cool lettuce is a perfect compliment to the spicy chicken. If you don't have lettuce, roll this mixture in flour tortillas, or serve it unwrapped over white rice.

1 TABLESPOON VEGETABLE OIL

1 TABLESPOON PLUS 1 TEASPOON SESAME OIL

1 TEASPOON CHOPPED FRESH GINGER

1 TEASPOON MINCED GARLIC

1 POUND BONELESS CHICKEN, DICED

1/2 CUP FINELY CHOPPED ONION

1/2 CUP DICED WATER CHESTNUTS

1/4 CUP GRATED CARROT

1/2 CUP DICED HAM

1 TABLESPOON SOY SAUCE

1 TABLESPOON HOISIN SAUCE

1/4 CUP CHICKEN BROTH MIXED WITH 2 TEASPOONS CORNSTARCH

12 WHOLE ICEBERG OR BIBB LETTUCE LEAVES, WASHED AND DRIED

Heat the vegetable oil and 1 tablespoon of the sesame oil over high heat in a wok or large skillet, add the ginger and garlic, and stir-fry for a few seconds. Add the chicken and stir-fry until the chicken turns white on all sides. Remove from the pan, and add the onion, water chestnuts, carrot, and ham. Stir-fry for 2 minutes, then return the chicken to the pan, tossing the mixture. Add the soy and Hoisin sauces, stirring until combined with the stir-fry mixture. Pour the broth mixture over the stir-fry and stir until thickened. Sprinkle with the remaining sesame oil and remove to a serving platter. Place 1 to 2 tablespoons of chicken in the center of each lettuce leaf. Tuck in the bottom and sides, gently rolling each package to encase the filling. Serve 2 per person.

Fresh veggie wrappers become more pliable for wrapping when left at room temperature for 30 minutes.

Blackened Snapper Wraps

SERVES 6

A little bit of Cajun and a lot of flavor go into these wraps. The fish is grilled with a light coating of Cajun spices, then wrapped in a tortilla with rice, artichoke hearts, and mushrooms in a creamy sauce. The rice and sauce are a perfect balance to the slightly spicy fish. If you are able to find spinach tortillas in your area, they make a great wrap for this dish.

1/4 CUP OLIVE OIL

3 TABLESPOONS CAJUN SEASONING (SEE RECIPE PAGE 86)

2 POUNDS RED SNAPPER FILLETS

2 TABLESPOONS BUTTER

2 15-OUNCE CANS ARTICHOKE HEARTS, DRAINED AND CHOPPED

1 CUP SLICED MUSHROOMS

SALT AND FRESHLY GROUND BLACK PEPPER TO TASTE

1 TABLESPOON LEMON JUICE

1/2 CUP HEAVY CREAM

6 TORTILLAS (12-INCH)

2 CUPS COOKED SOUTHWESTERN RICE (SEE RECIPE ON NEXT PAGE)

BABY GREENS FOR GARNISH

LEMON WEDGES FOR GARNISH

In a shallow bowl large enough to accommodate the snapper, combine the oil and Cajun seasoning. Dip the fish into the oil mixture and refrigerate until ready to grill. Preheat your oven's broiler. Broil the fish 4 inches from the flame for 5 to 7 minutes, or until the fish is cooked through. While the fish is cooking, melt the butter in a 10-inch sauté pan, and add the artichokes and mushrooms. Season with salt and pepper and the lemon juice. Sauté until the vegetables lose some of their liquid. Add the heavy cream and boil until the sauce thickens. Remove from the heat. Place a tortilla on each plate. Spread some of the rice in the center of each tortilla. Arrange a snapper fillet in the center of the tortilla, then top with some of the vegetable mixture. Beginning at the bottom of the tortilla, fold the tortilla up over the filling, bring in the two sides, then rolling from the bottom, roll over the filling to seal the package. Repeat until all wraps are completed. Serve each tortilla wrap on a bed of baby greens, garnished with lemon wedges.

Southwestern Rice

1 ONION, FINELY CHOPPED

1/2 CUP CHOPPED ANAHEIM CHILI PEPPER, SEEDED

2 RIBS CELERY, CHOPPED

1/2 TEASPOON GROUND CUMIN

1/2 TEASPOON DRIED OREGANO

1 TABLESPOON VEGETABLE OIL

1 CUP CHOPPED TOMATOES

1 CUP RAW LONG-GRAIN RICE

2 1/2 CUPS CHICKEN BROTH

In a 3-quart saucepan, cook the onion, chili pepper, celery, cumin, and oregano in the oil, until the vegetables are softened but not browned. Add the tomatoes, and allow to boil for 2 minutes. Add the rice, and stir to combine with the vegetables. Stir in the chicken broth, bring the mixture to a boil, then simmer covered for 15 to 20 minutes, or until the broth is absorbed. This rice keeps in the refrigerator for 5 days.

Cajun Seasoning Mix

Cajun spices are a blend that enhance the flavor of most foods, but especially seafood. Use this blend to spread on fish fillets before barbecueing, or add to seafood soups and stews.

3 TABLESPOONS SALT

1 TABLESPOON PAPRIKA

1 TABLESPOON ONION POWDER

1 TABLESPOON GARLIC POWDER

1 TABLESPOON CAYENNE PEPPER

$1/2$ TEASPOON WHITE PEPPER

2 TEASPOONS WHOLE DRIED THYME LEAVES

$1/2$ TEASPOON FRESHLY GROUND BLACK PEPPER

1 TEASPOON WHOLE DRIED OREGANO

Stir all the ingredients together in a small bowl, then store in an airtight jar for up to 6 months.

Breakfast Strudels

This is the perfect brunch dish. Flaky phyllo encases eggs and sausage in a sublime Swiss cheese sauce. These wraps can be assembled up to two months ahead and frozen, or refrigerated for 2 days. If you are watching your cholesterol, use egg substitute and turkey sausage in this recipe.

CHEESE SAUCE

1½ TABLESPOONS BUTTER

1½ TABLESPOONS FLOUR

¾ CUP MILK

6 TABLESPOONS GRATED SWISS CHEESE

2 TABLESPOONS GRATED PARMESAN CHEESE

¼ TEASPOON SALT

PINCH OF CAYENNE PEPPER

PINCH OF NUTMEG

Melt the butter over low heat in a small saucepan. Add the flour and whisk until smooth. Gradually whisk in the milk. Continue whisking until the mixture thickens and comes to a boil. Remove from the heat. Stir in the cheese and seasonings and pour into a medium bowl.

EGG-SAUSAGE MIXTURE

10 OUNCES PORK SAUSAGE MEAT (OR TURKEY SAUSAGE)

5 EGGS

½ TEASPOON DRIED THYME

FRESHLY GROUND BLACK PEPPER

1 TABLESPOON BUTTER

1 TABLESPOON MINCED FRESH PARSLEY

Cook the sausage in a small skillet over medium-high heat until it is no longer pink, breaking up with a fork as you cook it. Transfer to a colander and drain. In a separate bowl, mix the eggs, thyme, and pepper. Add the sausage to the egg mixture. Melt the butter in a 12-inch skillet or sauté pan over high heat. Add the egg mixture and stir with a fork until just set but still moist. Mix the eggs into the sauce, and stir in the parsley. Taste for seasoning, and refrigerate until the mixture is cold.

ASSEMBLY

¹/₂ **POUND PHYLLO DOUGH**	¹/₂ **CUP DRY BREAD CRUMBS**
1 **CUP (2 STICKS) MELTED BUTTER, COOLED**	**EGG-SAUSAGE FILLING**

Preheat the oven to 400°F. Line a baking sheet with aluminum foil. Arrange one phyllo sheet on the work surface. Keep remaining sheets covered with a kitchen towel. Brush the pastry sheet with melted butter and sprinkle with the bread crumbs. Fold the sheet in half lengthwise. Brush with butter, and spoon ¹/₃ cup filling on the short end of the pastry sheet. Fold the end of the pastry over the filling and fold in the edges. Brush the pastry with butter and, starting at the short end with the filling, fold the dough to form a package. Arrange seam-side down on a jelly-roll pan that has been lined with foil or parchment paper. Brush with additional butter. Continue until you have completed all the strudels. At this point, the packages may be wrapped airtight and frozen for up to 2 months, or they can be refrigerated for 2 days. When ready to serve, bake the strudels for 15 to 20 minutes at 400°F, until golden-brown. Serve immediately. Add 5 to 7 minutes to the cooking time if the strudels were frozen.

Broccoli, Mushroom, and Cheese Calzone

SERVES 6

A vegetarian delight, this calzone rolls up my favorite vegetables, binds them together with three cheeses, and forms a mouth-watering taste treat. When stuffing dough with vegetables, they tend to sweat a bit during the cooking time, so it is best to cook any veggies ahead of time, rendering most of the moisture, so that the dough remains crisp. Leftover chicken or fish is a delicious addition to this filling.

2 TABLESPOONS BUTTER

1 LARGE ONION, CHOPPED

2 CUPS SLICED MUSHROOMS

2 TABLESPOONS SHERRY

1 TEASPOON DRIED TARRAGON

SALT AND FRESHLY GROUND BLACK
PEPPER TO TASTE

4 CUPS COOKED BROCCOLI FLORETS

$^1/_2$ CUP GARLIC OIL

1 CUP GRATED MONTEREY JACK CHEESE

$^1/_2$ CUP GRATED GRUYÈRE

$^1/_2$ CUP GRATED PARMESAN CHEESE

1 RECIPE CALZONE DOUGH, ROLLED INTO
TWO 16-TO-18-INCH CIRCLES (SEE PAGE 133)

In a 10-inch sauté pan, melt the butter and add the onion and sliced mushrooms. Sauté for 3 to 5 minutes, until the mushrooms have given off most of their liquid. Add the sherry and toss the mushrooms over high heat, until the sherry has evaporated. Remove the skillet from the heat and add the tarragon, salt, and pepper. Transfer to a mixing bowl and allow to cool. Add the broccoli, 2 tablespoons of garlic oil, Monterey Jack cheese, Gruyère, and $^1/_4$ cup of the Parmesan cheese. Toss the mixture to combine. Brush the prepared dough with a thin coat of garlic oil, leaving a 1-inch border all the way around. Place half of the broccoli mixture on one-half of the first dough circle. Fold the dough over the filling and crimp the edges. Brush the top with additional garlic oil and sprinkle with Parmesan cheese. Repeat with the remaining dough. Bake the calzones in a preheated 350°F. oven for 20 to 25 minutes, or until they are golden-brown. Remove from the oven and let rest for 10 minutes before serving. Baked calzone can be frozen for 2 weeks, then reheated in a 400-degree oven for 15 to 20 minutes.

Making your own garlic oil is easy. I recommend making a small amount at a time. Soak 6 to 8 garlic cloves in vinegar overnight. Pour 1 cup of olive oil into a glass jar, bruise the garlic cloves and add them to the oil. Cover and let stand for 3 days. Remove the garlic cloves from the oil, strain, and refrigerate. The olive oil will solidify in the refrigerator; before using, remove from the refrigerator and zap in the microwave for 10 to 20 seconds. See Source Guide for garlic oil purveyors.

Carne Asada Fajitas

SERVES 6

A kind of build-your-own taco, fajitas feature grilled meats served in tortillas with condiments. Toppers for fajitas include fresh tomato salsa, guacamole, grated cheese, lettuce, and salsa verde. If you prefer chicken, follow the directions for the beef, substituting 3 whole boneless, skinless chicken breasts cut into 1/2-inch-wide strips. These wraps would make a perfect buffet dinner, with a selection of condiments, Southwestern Rice, and Black Beans Olé to accompany the fajitas.

1/2 CUP SOY SAUCE

1/4 CUP PLUS 2 TABLESPOONS VEGETABLE OIL

1 TABLESPOON LIME JUICE

1/4 TEASPOON FRESHLY GROUND BLACK PEPPER TO TASTE

3 GARLIC CLOVES, MINCED

2 POUNDS BEEF SIRLOIN, FILET MIGNON, OR FLANK STEAK, CUT ON THE DIAGONAL INTO THIN SLICES

1 LARGE ONION, THINLY SLICED

1 RED PEPPER, THINLY SLICED

1 GREEN PEPPER, THINLY SLICED

12 CORN OR FLOUR TORTILLAS

2 CUPS GUACAMOLE (SEE RECIPE, PAGE 39)

1 CUP FRESH TOMATO SALSA (SEE RECIPE, PAGE 38)

2 CUPS SHREDDED LETTUCE

2 CUPS GRATED COLBY OR MONTEREY JACK CHEESE

2 CUPS SOUR CREAM

In a zipper-type storage bag or shallow glass bowl, combine the soy sauce, 1/4 cup of the vegetable oil, the lime juice, pepper, and 1 clove of the minced garlic. Add the meat and marinate overnight. Heat the remaining 2 tablespoons of oil in a 12-inch sauté pan, and add the remaining minced garlic, onion, and the peppers. Sauté until the vegetables are softened. Remove from the pan. Drain the meat, then sauté in the same pan, until the meat is no longer pink. Add the pepper mixture and keep warm. Heat the tortillas.

Place two tortillas on each plate, layering with the meat-pepper mixture, guacamole, salsa, lettuce, cheese, and finishing with sour cream. Fold the tortillas over, as you would for a taco, and serve garnished with additional guacamole, salsa, and sour cream.

Chicken and Red Potato Wraps

SERVES 6

My grandmother's garlic and rosemary chicken recipe has been updated. Now the chicken is wrapped in potatoes, seasoned with a paste of roasted garlic, rosemary, and balsamic vinegar. This is a winner on a cold December night. I do not recommend using chicken breasts in this recipe because they will become dry during the long cooking process.

6 MEDIUM RED POTATOES, SCRUBBED AND CUT INTO ¼-INCH SLICES

½ CUP PLUS 3 TABLESPOONS OLIVE OIL

3 TABLESPOONS FRESH ROSEMARY

1 TEASPOON SALT

½ TEASPOON FRESHLY GROUND PEPPER

¼ CUP ROASTED GARLIC PASTE (SEE RECIPE, PAGE 93)

2 TABLESPOONS BALSAMIC VINEGAR

6 BONELESS, SKINLESS CHICKEN THIGHS

Place the red potatoes into a zipper-type storage bag and add the ½ cup of the olive oil, 1 tablespoon of the rosemary, and salt and pepper. Shake the bag to coat the potatoes. In a small bowl, combine the roasted garlic, the remaining rosemary and olive oil, and balsamic vinegar. Spread 1 to 2 tablespoons of this paste onto each chicken thigh. Line a jelly-roll pan with aluminum foil and brush with olive oil. Place 3 slices of potato on the pan as a base for each chicken thigh. Top the potatoes with a chicken thigh, and then cover the chicken with potatoes. (You may have more potatoes than you need, and if you do, just place them in an oiled serving dish to bake along with the chicken.) Brush any additional seasoned oil onto the potatoes. Preheat the oven to 400°F. Bake the chicken for 45 to 55 minutes, until the potatoes are golden-brown, and the chicken is cooked through. (By inserting a sharp knife into the chicken, you will see if the juices are pink or clear. If the juices are clear, the chicken is done.) Serve with a tossed green salad and crusty Italian bread.

Roasted Garlic

Roasted Garlic is mellow, and can be made at home in a toaster oven, or a conventional one. It keeps stored in the refrigerator for 2 weeks. Use roasted garlic to flavor wraps and sauces.

4 HEADS OF GARLIC **¼ CUP OLIVE OIL**

Cut off the top of the garlic, then place the head in an oven-proof dish. Sprinkle with 2 tablespoons oil and bake, covered with foil, at 350°F for 45 minutes. Remove the garlic from the oven and, using a pot holder, squeeze the garlic into a small jar or bowl. Mash the garlic and cover with the olive oil. Refrigerate until ready to use.

Chicken Parmesan Wraps

Serves 6

This dish makes an elegant entree for a dinner with family or friends. The chicken is precooked, covered with tomato sauce, grated Mozzarella cheese, then wrapped in phyllo that has been brushed with garlic butter and sprinkled with Parmesan cheese and fresh parsley. These wraps can be made 2 days ahead of time, then refrigerated, or they can be frozen for up to 6 weeks.

6¹/₂ CHICKEN BREASTS, SKINNED AND BONED

1 TEASPOON SALT

¹/₄ TEASPOON FRESHLY GROUND PEPPER

2 TABLESPOONS OLIVE OIL

¹/₂ POUND PHYLLO DOUGH

1 CUP (2 STICKS) MELTED BUTTER, COOLED

1 GARLIC CLOVE, MINCED

¹/₄ TEASPOON PAPRIKA

1 CUP GRATED PARMESAN CHEESE

¹/₄ CUP CHOPPED FRESH PARSLEY

1 CUP COLD TOMATO SAUCE (SEE EGGPLANT WRAPS, PAGE 102)

1 TABLESPOON DRIED OREGANO

1¹/₂ CUPS GRATED MOZZARELLA CHEESE

Preheat the oven to 400°F. Line a jelly-roll pan with foil or parchment. Sprinkle the chicken with salt and pepper. Heat the oil in a 12-inch sauté pan, and brown the chicken but do not cook through. Remove the chicken from the pan and cool. Cover the phyllo with a kitchen towel. Combine the butter with the garlic and paprika. Remove 1 sheet of phyllo and brush it with the garlic butter. Combine the parsley and Parmesan in a small bowl. Sprinkle one or two tablespoons over the phyllo. Layer another sheet of phyllo, brush with the butter, and sprinkle with cheese and parsley. Fold the phyllo in half widthwise. Place the cool chicken breast in the center of the phyllo, leaving 1 inch at the top. Brush with butter, sprinkle with the cheese/parsley mixture. Top the chicken with 1 to 2 tablespoons of cold Tomato Sauce. Sprinkle with oregano, then top with 2 tablespoons grated mozzarella. Fold the top of the phyllo over the chicken, fold in the sides, brush with butter, sprinkle with cheese and parsley, then roll up the wrap. Brush with butter, and sprinkle with additional cheese and parsley. Place the package, tomato sauce–side up, on the prepared pan and refrigerate for up to 2 days, or freeze for 6 weeks. When you are ready to serve, bake for 20 minutes, or until the phyllo is golden-brown.

Coco Loco Quesadilla

This wrap is my daughter Carrie's favorite. The sauce and chicken can be prepared 2 days ahead of time, and the quesadilla is heated just before serving. Recycling your leftover chicken into this wrap will make your family forget they had chicken the night before.

1 TABLESPOON VEGETABLE OIL	2 CANS TOMATO PUREE (16-OUNCE)
1 ONION, SLICED THINLY	1/2 CUP CHICKEN BROTH
1 RED PEPPER, CORED, THINLY SLICED	4 CUPS COOKED CHICKEN, CUT INTO STRIPS
1 GREEN PEPPER, CORED, THINLY SLICED	
3 GARLIC CLOVES, MINCED	6 LARGE TORTILLAS
2 TABLESPOONS CHILI POWDER	4 CUPS GRATED MONTEREY JACK CHEESE
1 TEASPOON GROUND CUMIN	SOUR CREAM AND ADDITIONAL GRATED MONTEREY JACK CHEESE FOR GARNISH

Heat the oil in a 5-quart stock pot. Add the onion, peppers, garlic, chili powder, and cumin. Cook over medium-high heat for about 5 minutes, until the vegetables are softened. Add the tomato puree and the chicken broth, stirring up any of the vegetables that may be stuck to the bottom of the pan. Simmer uncovered for 45 minutes. Taste for seasoning and adjust. Add the chicken to the sauce, and simmer for another 30 minutes. The sauce can be refrigerated for up to 3 days, or frozen for 1 month. Place 1 tortilla in a 12-inch sauté pan, and cover with a layer of grated cheese. Heat on medium until the cheese begins to melt, then fold the quesadilla in half, heating until the cheese is melted. Repeat with remaining 5 tortillas. Remove to a serving plate and cover with the sauce. Serve garnished with sour cream and additional grated cheese.

Confetti Philly Steak Wraps

SERVES 6

Anyone who has ever been to Philadelphia has doubtless tasted that staple found in every neighborhood eatery: the Philly cheesesteak sandwich. Thin strips of steak are grilled with onions and peppers, then topped with cheese and stuffed into an Italian roll. There are debates about what kind of cheese, if there should be mushrooms, and what color peppers to use. This lighter version, with less bread and not so much cheese, is a wrap that may just satisfy all those from the City of Brotherly Love. Featuring red, green, and yellow peppers, sautéed with red onion and mushrooms, the steak is marinated and then quickly stir-fried, popped into a pita, and covered with the multicolored pepper and onion mixture. It makes a terrific wrap worthy of applause, or at least the ringing of the Liberty Bell!

2 POUNDS STEAK, CUT ON THE DIAGONAL INTO THIN STRIPS

1/4 CUP LIGHT SOY SAUCE

2 TABLESPOONS VEGETABLE OIL

1 GARLIC CLOVE, MINCED

1 TABLESPOON WHITE WINE

1 TABLESPOON PLUS 1 TEASPOON SUGAR

1 LARGE RED PEPPER, WASHED, SEEDED, AND THINLY SLICED

1 LARGE YELLOW PEPPER, WASHED, SEEDED, AND THINLY SLICED

1 LARGE GREEN PEPPER, WASHED, SEEDED, AND THINLY SLICED

1 CUP THINLY SLICED RED ONION

1 CUP SLICED MUSHROOMS

2 TEASPOONS SALT

1/2 TEASPOON FRESHLY GROUND PEPPER

1 TEASPOON DRIED OREGANO

1 CUP GRATED MONTEREY JACK CHEESE (OPTIONAL)

6 PITAS

Trim the steak of any fat, and slice thinly into strips. In a glass bowl, combine the soy sauce, 1 tablespoon of the oil, garlic, white wine, and 1 teaspoon of the sugar. Add the beef, and stir to coat the meat. Refrigerate for 30 minutes, or up to 8 hours. In a 10- or 12-inch skillet, heat the oil over high heat, then add the peppers, onion, and mushrooms. Cook over high heat, tossing the vegetables, adding the salt, pepper, and the remaining sugar, stirring constantly. Continue to cook for about 5 minutes, or until the vegetables are crisp but tender. Season the mixture with oregano, then set aside.

Drain the steak from the marinade. Heat a wok on high, then add the steak, stir-frying until it loses its pink color. Remove from the heat. Cut the pitas in half, and open each pocket. Place some of the steak into each pocket, cover with some of the Monterey Jack cheese if used, and then top with the pepper and mushroom mixture. Serve 2 halves per person.

To mince garlic: Investing in a garlic press is an excellent idea. There are several self-cleaning models that do a wonderful job of mashing garlic, but if the cloves are tough then continue to mince the garlic into a paste on a cutting board with the back of a knife or a metal pastry scraper.

To mince the garlic by hand, peel the garlic, then with the flat part of a wide blade knife, smash the garlic clove onto a flat work surface. Taking the knife, mince the garlic, then puree it with the flat of the knife. Adding salt to the garlic helps to soften it.

Another way is to place the garlic between two pieces of waxed paper and pound it with the flat part of a meat tenderizer or with a wine bottle.

Covent Garden Market Wraps

SERVES 6

The Market Cafe in London serves this bit of springtime all year long. Ham and asparagus are wrapped with Swiss cheese sauce in phyllo dough, then set in a pool of Cucumber Hollandaise sauce. The wraps can be made 2 days in advance and refrigerated or frozen, for one month, but the Cucumber Hollandaise should be made just before serving.

2 TABLESPOONS BUTTER

2 TABLESPOONS ALL-PURPOSE FLOUR

1 CUP MILK

1/2 CUP GRATED SWISS CHEESE

DASH OF NUTMEG

1/2 POUND PHYLLO DOUGH

1 CUP (2 STICKS) BUTTER, MELTED

1/2 CUP DRY BREAD CRUMBS

12 SLICES CANADIAN BACON (1/2 INCH THICK)

18 ASPARAGUS TIPS, BLANCHED

ADDITIONAL ASPARAGUS TIPS OR SLICED CUCUMBERS FOR GARNISH

In a small saucepan, melt the butter, add the flour, and whisk until the flour is incorporated. Stir the flour until white bubbles form, gradually add the milk, and whisking until the mixture is smooth and thick. Remove from the heat and add the Swiss cheese and nutmeg, stirring until the cheese is melted. Refrigerate the sauce until thick and cold.

Unwrap and cover the phyllo with a kitchen towel. Remove 1 sheet of phyllo from the stack and place on a flat work surface. Brush with melted butter, sprinkle with some bread crumbs, and layer another sheet over the top. Brush with butter and sprinkle crumbs over the second sheet. Fold the phyllo in half widthwise, and brush with butter. Place two slices Canadian bacon in the center of the wrap, top with three spears of asparagus, and 2 tablespoons of sauce. Bringing in the four corners, twist the phyllo around the ham and asparagus. Brush with additional butter and place on a jelly-roll pan that has been lined with parchment or foil. Continue until you have assembled 6 wraps. Refrigerate for up 2 days, or freeze for 1 month.

When ready to serve, preheat the oven to 400°F. Bake the wraps for 15 minutes, or until golden. Remove from the oven, place 3 tablespoons Cucumber Hollandaise in the center of each plate, and center the wrap on the sauce. Garnish with additional asparagus or with sliced cucumbers.

Cucumber Hollandaise

3 EGG YOLKS

2 TABLESPOONS FRESH SQUEEZED LEMON JUICE

¹/₂ TEASPOON DRY MUSTARD

¹/₂ TEASPOON SALT

³/₄ CUP (1¹/₂ STICKS) HOT MELTED BUTTER

2 TABLESPOONS FINELY CHOPPED FRESH PARSLEY

1 TABLESPOON FINELY CHOPPED FRESH CHIVES

¹/₂ CUP CUCUMBER, PEELED, SEEDED, AND DICED

Place the yolks, lemon juice, mustard, and salt in a blender, or the work bowl of a food processor. With the motor running, gradually add the hot butter through the feed tube until the sauce thickens. Taste for seasoning, and add additional salt or lemon juice, blending once more. Remove from the work bowl, and add the parsley, chives, and cucumber. Keep warm in the top of a double boiler or in a thermos.

*When your **French baguettes** are too hard to do anything else with, process them in the food processor, or place them in a zipper-type storage bag and run a rolling pin over them. You'll have high-quality bread crumbs for a fraction of the cost of store-bought crumbs. Once the crumbs are done, place them in a storage bag in the freezer for the next time you work with phyllo or need to bread chicken cutlets.*

Curried Chicken and Shrimp Wraps

SERVES 6

Wraps are best when they are bursting with flavors, and this one is a great example of simple cooking elevated to the next level. Curried chicken and shrimp is wrapped in tortillas containing rice and a flavorful Chutney Salad. The curry can be made 2 days ahead and reheated just before serving. The salad dressing keeps in the refrigerator for 2 weeks.

CURRIED CHICKEN AND SHRIMP

3 TABLESPOONS BUTTER

2 TEASPOONS CURRY POWDER

$^1/_2$ CUP CHOPPED ONION

1 APPLE, CORED AND CHOPPED (LEAVE THE PEEL ON)

3 TABLESPOONS ALL-PURPOSE FLOUR

$1^3/_4$ CUPS CHICKEN BROTH

$^1/_4$ CUP HEAVY CREAM

2 CUPS COOKED CHICKEN, CUT INTO 1-INCH DICE

1 CUP COOKED MEDIUM-SIZED SHRIMP, PEELED AND DEVEINED

In a 3-quart saucepan, melt the butter, and add the curry powder, onion, and apple. Sauté for 3 minutes, then add the flour. Stir until the flour is incorporated. Gradually add the chicken broth, whisking until smooth. Add the cream, bring to a boil, then add the chicken and shrimp. Refrigerate the curry mixture up to 2 days before serving.

Chutney Salad

$^1/_4$ CUP MAJOR GREY'S CHUTNEY

$^1/_4$ CUP RICE WINE VINEGAR

$^1/_3$ CUP VEGETABLE OIL

1 GARLIC CLOVE, MINCED

6 CUPS THINLY SLICED ICEBERG LETTUCE

4 SLICES RED ONION

$^1/_2$ CUP GOLDEN RAISINS (OPTIONAL)

$^1/_4$ CUP CHOPPED PEANUTS

In a blender or the work bowl of the food processor, blend the chutney, vinegar, oil, and garlic until it emulsifies. Place the lettuce, onion, raisins, and peanuts into a salad bowl. Pour the dressing over the lettuce, and toss to coat.

ASSEMBLY

12 SMALL FLOUR TORTILLAS

3 CUPS JASMINE RICE (SEE RECIPE, PAGE 120)

3–4 CUPS CURRIED CHICKEN AND SHRIMP

6½ CUPS CHUTNEY SALAD

FLAKED COCONUT, CHOPPED PEANUTS, RAISINS, AND/OR CHOPPED TOMATOES FOR GARNISH

Place 2 tortillas on each dinner plate. Arrange ¹/₄ cup Jasmine Rice down the center of the tortillas. Cover with ¹/₃ cup of the curry, and top with some of the Chutney Salad. Roll up the tortillas, and garnish the plate with coconut, chopped peanuts, raisins, and/or chopped tomatoes.

Eggplant Wraps

This is a delicious vegetarian entree that resembles eggplant Parmesan. Eggplant is sautéed, stuffed with a cheese-and-bread-crumb mixture, then covered with tomato sauce and grated cheese. The wraps can be made 2 days ahead of time, and refrigerated or frozen for 2 months.

2 TABLESPOONS OLIVE OIL

1 LARGE EGGPLANT, PEELED AND SLICED LENGTHWISE INTO $^1/_2$-INCH PIECES

1 $^1/_2$ CUPS SOFT BREAD CRUMBS

1 CUP GRATED PARMESAN CHEESE

2 EGGS

2 TABLESPOONS CHOPPED FRESH PARSLEY

$^1/_2$ TEASPOON FRESHLY GROUND BLACK PEPPER

TOMATO SAUCE (RECIPE ON NEXT PAGE)

1 CUP GRATED MOZZARELLA CHEESE

Heat the oil in a 12-inch skillet over medium heat. Add the eggplant, a few slices at a time, browning each side. Remove to paper towels to drain, adding additional oil to the pan, as needed, until all the eggplant is cooked. In a small bowl, mix together the bread crumbs, $^1/_2$ cup of the Parmesan, eggs, parsley, and ground pepper. Place 2 tablespoons of the filling across the center of each eggplant slice. Roll up the eggplant, placing the rolls in a 13 × 9-inch ovenproof baking dish that has been spread with $^1/_2$ cup Tomato Sauce. Cover the rolls with tomato sauce, mozzarella, and the remaining Parmesan cheese. Bake in a preheated 350-degree oven for 30 to 45 minutes, or until the cheese is melted and bubbling.

Tomato Sauce

A great all-purpose sauce, keep it in the freezer for unexpected company; add meatballs, vegetables, or seafood, and serve over pasta.

¼ CUP OLIVE OIL

1 CLOVE GARLIC, MINCED

½ CUP CHOPPED ONION

3 CUPS CHOPPED CANNED PLUM TOMATOES

1 TABLESPOON FRESH BASIL (OR 1 TEA-SPOON DRIED—IF YOU PLAN TO FREEZE THE SAUCE, USE DRIED)

1 TABLESPOON CHOPPED FRESH PARSLEY

½ TEASPOON SALT

¼ TEASPOON FRESHLY GROUND BLACK PEPPER

1 TABLESPOON SUGAR

Heat the oil in a 3-quart saucepan, adding the garlic and onion. Sauté the vegetables until they are softened. Add the tomatoes, herbs, and seasonings, and cook uncovered for 30 minutes. Taste the sauce and season with additional salt and pepper. The sauce can be refrigerated for 3 days or frozen for two months.

Falafel Wraps

In the Eastern Mediterranean falafel is the fast food of choice. As popular as hamburgers are in this country, these small cakes are made with chickpeas and seasonings, placed on a griddle or fried, then tucked into a pita and served with a sesame-flavored sour cream sauce, or mild cucumber yogurt sauce (see Chicken Kabob Wraps). The falafel can be prepared earlier in the day, refrigerated, or frozen for up to one month. A quick warmup in the microwave or a hot oven will have dinner on the table in less time than you think.

2 CUPS FRESH, SOFT BREAD CRUMBS

¹/₂ CUP CHOPPED FRESH PARSLEY

1 TABLESPOON GREEK SEASONING (SEE RECIPE, PAGE 106)

1 20-OUNCE CAN CHICKPEAS, RINSED AND DRAINED

¹/₂ CUP CHOPPED ONION

1 LARGE CLOVE GARLIC, MINCED

1 EGG

1 TABLESPOON SESAME OIL

¹/₂ CUP FLOUR

¹/₂ CUP VEGETABLE OIL

6 PITAS

SESAME SOUR CREAM SAUCE (SEE RECIPE NEXT PAGE)

2 CUPS SHREDDED LETTUCE

1 CUP CHOPPED FRESH TOMATOES

LEMON SLICES AND PARSLEY SPRIGS FOR GARNISH

In a food processor fitted with a steel blade, combine the bread crumbs, parsley, seasoning, chickpeas, onion, garlic, egg, and sesame oil. Process for 30 seconds, scrape down the bowl, and process for another 10 seconds. Transfer to a mixing bowl, and refrigerate for 1 hour to firm. When ready to serve, form the falafel mixture into patties, about 2 inches in diameter. Heat the vegetable oil over high heat, and dust each patty with some of the flour. Fry the patties for 2 minutes on each side, until golden. Drain on paper toweling. Place 2 patties on each pita, top with Sesame Sour Cream Sauce (or Cucumber Yogurt Sauce, page 111), and sprinkle with some of the lettuce and chopped tomatoes. Serve immediately, garnished with lemon slices and parsley sprigs.

Sesame Sour Cream Sauce

2 CUPS SOUR CREAM

1/2 CUP TAHINI

1 TABLESPOON FRESH LEMON JUICE

1/2 TEASPOON SALT

1/2 TEASPOON DRIED THYME

1/8 TEASPOON FRESHLY GROUND PEPPER

1/4 TEASPOON DRIED OREGANO

Combine the ingredients in a small glass bowl. Stir to soften the tahini, and then whisk the sauce until smooth. Store in the refrigerator for up to one week. This makes a great dip for pita as well as a topping for the falafel.

Greek Seasoning

Making your own Greek seasoning blend is simple, and the mixture can be stored in airtight jars for up to 6 months. Try mixing this into ground beef or turkey for great burgers and meatloaf, or blend it with lemon juice and olive oil for a wonderful chicken marinade. This makes a great hostess gift, when you give it in a pretty spice jar or canister, with a favorite recipe attached.

2 TABLESPOONS SALT

2 TEASPOONS PAPRIKA

1 TEASPOON FRESHLY GROUND BLACK PEPPER

2 TEASPOONS GRANULATED GARLIC POWDER (TRY THE VARIETIES FOUND IN HEALTH FOOD STORES)

2 TEASPOONS DRIED OREGANO

1 TABLESPOON DRIED PARSLEY

1/2 TEASPOON DRIED LEMON PEEL

Combine all the ingredients in a small bowl and stir to blend. Store the seasoning in an airtight jar.

Grilled Fish Tacos Especial

SERVES 6

*Fish tacos originated in the Baja California fishing village of San
Felipe. Street vendors load deep-fried fish, white and red salsa,
shredded cabbage, and cheese into warmed corn tortillas. For a
lighter taste, grilled fish is topped with cabbage salad, guacamole,
and a sprinkle of grated Monterey Jack cheese. Serve a choice of tortillas, and if you are adventuresome, let your guests roll their own
by placing all the ingredients on a counter and serving buffet style.*

FISH

¹/₄ CUP VEGETABLE OIL

2 TABLESPOONS FRESH LIME JUICE

¹/₂ TEASPOON GROUND BLACK PEPPER

2 POUNDS FIRM WHITE-FLESHED FISH
(SUCH AS A SEA BASS, SNAPPER, OR
MAKO SHARK)

Combine the oil, lime juice, and pepper in a glass baking dish. Add the fish and allow
it to marinate in the refrigerator for about 30 minutes. Heat a charcoal grill until the
coals have formed a white ash, or preheat the broiler. Grill the fish 4 inches from
the heat source, a total of 10 minutes for each inch of thickness. Remove the fish
from the grill; it is ready to serve.

South-of-the-Border Cabbage Salad

2 CUPS SHREDDED GREEN CABBAGE
(1 SMALL HEAD)

$^1/_2$ CUP SHREDDED RED CABBAGE

$^1/_3$ CUP VEGETABLE OIL

2 TABLESPOONS FRESH LIME JUICE

1 TEASPOON SUGAR

2 TEASPOONS CHOPPED CILANTRO

$^1/_2$ TEASPOON SALT

$^1/_4$ TEASPOON FRESHLY GROUND BLACK
PEPPER

Combine the cabbages in a glass bowl. Whisk together the oil, lime juice, sugar, cilantro, and salt and pepper. Pour over the cabbage and toss until blended. Refrigerate the salad for up to 8 hours before serving.

White Salsa

$^1/_4$ CUP FRESH TOMATO SALSA, DRAINED
(SEE RECIPE, PAGE 38)

2 CUPS SOUR CREAM, OR NONFAT YOGURT

1 BUNCH FRESH CILANTRO, CHOPPED FOR
GARNISH

Combine the Salsa and sour cream in a bowl, whisking until blended. Garnish with fresh cilantro.

ASSEMBLY

12 TORTILLAS (6-INCH)

2 POUNDS GRILLED FISH

$2^1/_4$ CUPS WHITE SALSA

$2^1/_2$ CUPS SOUTH-OF-THE-BORDER
CABBAGE SALAD

2 CUPS GUACAMOLE (SEE RECIPE, PAGE 39)

2 CUPS GRATED MONTEREY JACK CHEESE

CHOPPED FRESH CILANTRO FOR GARNISH

LIME WEDGES FOR GARNISH

On a flat surface or serving plate, arrange 2 tortillas. Place grilled fish in the center of the tortilla, then top with white salsa, cabbage salad, Guacamole, and cheese. Serve garnished with chopped cilantro and lime wedges.

Kebab Wraps

SERVES 6

My favorite Greek café serves this wonderful chicken wrap in pita, then dresses it with Greek salad and a special cucumber yogurt dressing. The chicken marinade is equally good for roasting whole chicken, giving it a lemony glaze.

Chicken Kebabs

¼ CUP OLIVE OIL

2 TABLESPOONS LEMON JUICE

ZEST OF ½ LEMON

1 TEASPOON DRIED OREGANO

½ TEASPOON DRIED THYME

2 GARLIC CLOVES, MINCED

1 TEASPOON SALT

½ TEASPOON FRESHLY GROUND BLACK PEPPER

DASH OF HOT PEPPER SAUCE

2 WHOLE CHICKEN BREASTS, CUT INTO 1-INCH KEBAB CHUNKS

6 LARGE PITAS

In a glass mixing bowl, whisk together the oil, lemon juice, lemon zest, oregano, thyme, garlic, salt and pepper, and hot sauce. Marinate the chicken pieces in the sauce for about 1 hour. Thread the chicken chunks on skewers, and grill 4 inches away from the flame for 4 to 8 minutes, or until done. Baste with additional marinade during the cooking time. Remove the chicken from the skewers.

Greek Salad

4 CUPS TORN ASSORTED LEAF LETTUCES

1/2 CUP CHOPPED CUCUMBER

1/2 CUP SLICED RED ONION

1/2 CUP PITTED KALAMATA OLIVES

1/4 CUP RED WINE VINEGAR

1/3 CUP OLIVE OIL

1 TEASPOON DRIED OREGANO

1/2 TEASPOON SALT

1/4 TEASPOON FRESHLY GROUND BLACK PEPPER

1/4 CUP CRUMBLED FETA CHEESE

Place the lettuce, cucumber, red onion, and olives into a salad bowl. In a glass jar or mixing bowl, combine the vinegar, oil, oregano, salt and pepper, and feta. Whisk to blend. Pour some of the dressing over the salad, and toss to coat. Add more dressing, if desired.

Lay one of the pitas on a flat work surface. Arrange 4 to 5 pieces of chicken down the center of the pita, top with 2 tablespoons of Cucumber Yogurt Sauce, then cover with salad. Roll up the pita, and secure with two toothpicks on each end. Repeat with remaining bread.

Lemon zest *can be easily removed with a swivel peeler.*
Take long strips of zest, and cut into tiny dices, or chop
in the mini-chopper. Freeze zest in zipper-type bags.

Cucumber Yogurt Sauce

MAKES 3 CUPS

Used extensively in Greek kitchens, this delicious sauce is good on just about everything, and can be used as a dip for raw veggies, too.

2 MEDIUM CUCUMBERS

³/₄ TEASPOON SALT

1 TABLESPOON WHITE VINEGAR

1 CLOVE GARLIC, MINCED

2 TABLESPOONS SNIPPED FRESH DILL

2 CUPS PLAIN YOGURT

1 TABLESPOON OLIVE OIL

Peel the cucumbers and halve lengthwise. Remove the seeds from the center of the cucumbers, and then grate. Place in a bowl, sprinkle with the salt, and refrigerate for one hour. In another bowl, stir together the vinegar, garlic, dill, yogurt, and olive oil. Drain the cucumbers and add to the yogurt mixture. Refrigerate for at least 4 hours before serving. This makes a delicious topping for kebabs or chicken wraps.

Korean Beef Rolls

*On my first trip to Korea I fell in love with the national beef dish,
Bulgoki. Marinated strips of meat are brought to the table with
condiments ranging from leafy green vegetables and spicy kimchee to rice and bean sprouts. The meat is grilled at your table
and wrapped in toasted nori with condiments. This meal is perfect
for family and friends who want to get involved in their food.
Place all the condiments and wraps on a Lazy Susan in the middle of the table or have each guest help themselves from a buffet
counter. For those guests who are skittish about wrapping in nori,
I recommend you use fresh lettuce leaves or flour tortillas.*

COOKED BEEF

2 POUNDS BEEF SIRLOIN OR FLANK STEAK, THINLY SLICED, ON THE DIAGONAL

1/2 CUP SOY SAUCE

1/4 CUP SUGAR

3 GARLIC CLOVES, MINCED

2 TEASPOONS MIRIN OR RICE WINE (OR SUBSTITUTE SHERRY)

2 TABLESPOONS SESAME OIL

2 TABLESPOONS SESAME SEEDS

1 TABLESPOON VEGETABLE OIL

Place the beef into a zipper-type storage bag or a glass bowl. In a small bowl, combine the remaining ingredients, save for the vegetable oil, stirring to dissolve the sugar. Pour over the beef and marinate overnight. When you are ready to serve the meat, drain it from the marinade. Heat the oil in a wok or 12-inch sauté pan. Add the meat a few pieces at a time, turning when one side is done. Remove the cooked meat to a heated serving platter.

Seoul Spinach

In Korea they use leafy vegetables similar to broccoli rabe and collards for this dish, but I am substituting spinach because it is more widely available here in the United States. Feel free to use your favorite leafy green in this recipe.

8 QUARTS WATER

2 POUNDS SPINACH, WASHED AND DRIED, TOUGH STEMS REMOVED

2 TABLESPOONS VEGETABLE OIL

1 TABLESPOON SESAME OIL

2 CLOVES GARLIC, CUT IN HALVES

1 TEASPOON SALT

$^{1}/_{2}$ TEASPOON FRESHLY GROUND PEPPER

1 TABLESPOON FRESH LEMON JUICE

2 TABLESPOONS SESAME SEEDS

Bring 8 quarts of water to a boil in a large stock pot. Plunge the spinach into the pot, and turn off the heat. Let the spinach sit for 3 minutes, remove from the water, and drain. Heat the oils in a wok or sauté pan. Add the garlic, sautéing for 3 to 5 minutes. Do not let the garlic brown. Remove the garlic and add the spinach to the flavored oil, stirring to coat. Add the salt, pepper, lemon juice, and sesame seeds, stirring to blend. Remove the spinach from the heat, and serve at room temperature.

Kimchee American Style

Kimchee is a fermented cabbage dish served at almost every meal in Korea. Spicy, sometimes sharp, I have taken some of the fire out of it for our tastes.

5 QUARTS WATER

1 MEDIUM HEAD CABBAGE, CUT INTO CHUNKS (DISCARD THE TOUGH OUTER LEAVES AND THE CORE)

$^{1}/_{3}$ CUP RICE WINE VINEGAR

$^{1}/_{2}$ CUP SUGAR

1 TABLESPOON HOT PEPPER FLAKES

1 TABLESPOON SOY SAUCE

1 TEASPOON SALT

$^{1}/_{4}$ CUP SESAME OIL

Bring 5 quarts of water to a boil in a stock pot. Add the cabbage to the water, and boil for 1 minute. Remove the cabbage from the water, and drain. In a serving bowl, combine the vinegar, sugar, hot pepper flakes, soy sauce, salt, and oil. Add the cabbage and mix together. Cover and chill for 2 days. Serve with Korean Beef Rolls (see recipe, page 112).

Sweet Hot Cucumber Salad

1 HOT HOUSE CUCUMBER

2 SCALLIONS (GREEN ONIONS), CHOPPED

1/2 CUP RICE VINEGAR

2 TABLESPOONS SUGAR

1/2 TEASPOON SALT

1/8 TEASPOON RED PEPPER FLAKES

Peel the cucumber and cut into 1/2-inch slices. Place the cucumber slices and scallions into a serving bowl. In another bowl whisk together the vinegar, sugar, salt, and red pepper flakes. Pour over the cucumber mixture, then toss to coat. Refrigerate for up to 3 days before serving.

ASSEMBLY

6 SHEETS TOASTED NORI (OR 6 FLOUR TORTILLAS)

2 CUPS COOKED SHORT GRAIN RICE

2 POUNDS COOKED BEEF

2 CUPS SEOUL SPINACH

4 CUPS KIMCHEE AMERICAN STYLE

2 CUPS SWEET HOT CUCUMBER SALAD

Lay the nori onto a work surface, and spread a layer of rice over it. Top with the beef, spinach, a bit of the kimchee (be careful), and some cucumber salad. Roll the nori and cut into 3 pieces. Serve additional spinach, kimchee, and cucumber salad on the side.

Mango Snapper Wraps

*Inspired by a dinner I once had in Maui, these wraps were origi-
nally made with Hawaiian escolar, but since snapper is more
readily available here, I've substituted it. The mild fish is grilled,
then paired with a sweet hot salsa and garnished with match-
stick–sized sweet potatoes fried and wrapped in corn tortillas. The
crispy sweet potatoes give a wonderful texture to this dish, so
don't leave them out!*

4 CUPS PLUS 1 TABLESPOON VEGETABLE OIL

1 TEASPOON CAJUN SEASONING (SEE PAGE 86)

1 1/2 POUNDS RED SNAPPER FILLETS (OR SUBSTITUTE ANY WHITE, FIRM-FLESHED FISH)

1 LARGE SWEET POTATO, CUT INTO 1/4-INCH × 2-INCH MATCHSTICKS

SALT TO TASTE

12 WARM CORN TORTILLAS

1 CUP MANGO SALSA (SEE RECIPE, PAGE 116)

FRESH FRUIT AND CHOPPED FRESH CILANTRO FOR GARNISH

Mix together 1 tablespoon of the oil and the Cajun Seasoning in a shallow dish. Dip the snapper fillets into the oil, coating the fish. Heat a 12-inch sauté pan on high, then sauté the fillets until they are done, about 3 minutes on each side. Remove the fillets from the pan and keep warm.

Heat the remaining oil in a deep-sided pan or deep-fat fryer. Add the sweet potato sticks and fry until crisp. Drain the potatoes on paper towels and sprinkle with salt to taste. Place 2 corn tortillas on each plate. Filling the tortillas as you would tacos, arrange some fish in each tortilla, cover with 1/4 cup Mango Salsa, and top with some of the potatoes. Serve garnished with fresh fruit and chopped fresh cilantro.

Mango Salsa

MAKES 2$^{1}/_{2}$ CUPS

Sweet, hot, and spicy, this delicious salsa complements grilled fish or chicken.

2 CUPS CHOPPED MANGO

1 GARLIC CLOVE, CRUSHED

$^{1}/_{2}$ CUP CHOPPED JALAPEÑO PEPPER

1 TABLESPOON CHOPPED FRESH CILANTRO

1 TEASPOON CHOPPED FRESH PARSLEY

$^{1}/_{4}$ CUP CHOPPED SCALLIONS (GREEN ONION)

$^{1}/_{3}$ CUP SUGAR

$^{1}/_{4}$ CUP WHITE VINEGAR

2 TABLESPOONS LIME JUICE

In a glass mixing bowl, combine the mango, garlic, jalapeño, cilantro, parsley, and scallions. Combine the sugar, vinegar, and lime juice in a nonreactive saucepan and bring to a boil, stirring to dissolve the sugar. Pour over the mango mixture and toss. Refrigerate for at least 6 hours before serving.

Mangoes are plentiful in the summertime, so buy them when they are at the peak season. Cut the mangoes into chunks and freeze in zipper-type storage bags in the freezer. They will keep for 6 months, so that in the dead of winter you can take them out and whip up Mango Salsa to bring some sunshine into a dreary day.

Omelette Wraps

A great way to get your guests involved in the preparation of breakfast or brunch, omelette wraps are easy, with fillings prepared ahead of time, then eggs cooked at the last minute. I have included my favorite fillings, but feel free to let your imagination run wild. If you are looking for a way to lower the cholesterol in this recipe, feel free to use an equivalent amount of egg substitute, or 6 whole eggs and 8 egg whites. A non-stick sauté or omelette pan will guarantee success with this recipe.

12 LARGE EGGS

¹/₄ CUP WATER

2 TEASPOONS SALT

1 TEASPOON FRESHLY GROUND BLACK PEPPER

1 TEASPOON BUTTER PER OMELETTE (6 TEASPOONS TOTAL), OR NON-STICK COOKING SPRAY

Break the eggs into a mixing bowl, add the water, salt, and pepper, whisking until smooth. Refrigerate until ready to make the omelettes. When ready to serve, heat a 10-inch non-stick sauté or omelette pan over medium-high heat. Add 1 teaspoon of butter, tilting the pan as it melts. The butter will foam, and when the foam seems to dissipate, add a scant ¹/₂ cup of the egg mixture. Shake the pan to distribute the egg. Lower the temperature to medium and allow the bottom of the egg mixture to set. Add your choice of topping, and fold in the top and bottom of the omelette. Cook another few minutes until the eggs are set. Using a long spatula, remove the omelette to a serving plate.

Bacon, Mushroom, Tomato Filling

If you would like to use turkey bacon or Canadian bacon instead
of regular bacon, sauté it in 1 tablespoon butter or margarine.

6 STRIPS BACON, CUT INTO ¹/₂-INCH
PIECES

¹/₂ CUP CHOPPED ONION

1 CUP SLICED MUSHROOMS

2 CUPS CHOPPED FRESH TOMATOES

1 TEASPOON THYME

2 TABLESPOONS CHOPPED FRESH PARSLEY

¹/₂ TEASPOON FRESHLY GROUND BLACK
PEPPER

In a 10-inch sauté pan, cook the bacon until it is crisp. Add the onions and mushrooms, sautéing for 5 minutes. Add the tomatoes and seasonings, and cook uncovered over medium heat for 15 minutes. This filling can be used to fill an omelette, or as a sauce for a plain egg omelette.

Veggie Bonanza

2 TABLESPOONS OLIVE OIL

¹/₂ CUP THINLY SLICED ONIONS

1 RED PEPPER, THINLY SLICED

2 MEDIUM ZUCCHINI, CUT INTO 2-INCH
MATCHSTICKS

1 CUP SLICED MUSHROOMS

1 TABLESPOON LEMON JUICE

2 TABLESPOONS FRESH SNIPPED DILL

¹/₂ TEASPOON SALT

¹/₄ TEASPOON FRESHLY GROUND PEPPER

1 CUP GRATED CHEDDAR CHEESE (OR
SUBSTITUTE SWISS, MONTEREY JACK,
PARMESAN, OR MOZZARELLA)

Heat the oil in a sauté pan and add the vegetables, cooking over medium-high heat until they are crisp but tender. Add the lemon juice, dill, salt, and pepper, stirring to combine. When adding to the omelette, place some of the filling on the center of the egg, cover with the cheese, and then fold the omelette.

Salmon Florentine

5 QUARTS BOILING WATER

4 CUPS FRESH SPINACH, CLEANED AND
DRIED

2 TABLESPOONS BUTTER

1/2 CUP CHOPPED ONION

2 CUPS COOKED SALMON

1/2 CUP HEAVY CREAM

1/8 TEASPOON NUTMEG

1 TEASPOON SALT

1/4 CUP GRATED GRUYÈRE OR IMPORTED
SWISS CHEESE

Plunge the spinach into 5 quarts of boiling water. Remove from the heat, drain, and squeeze dry of all moisture. Melt the butter in a 12-inch skillet, add the onion and spinach, sautéing until the vegetables soften. Add the salmon, heavy cream, spinach, nutmeg, and salt, bringing the mixture to a boil. Reduce the heat to simmer, and add the cheese. Keep warm until ready to serve.

Peking Duck Wraps

SERVES 6

Duck is one of those dishes that you may not make very often, but it is simple, and the results are delicious. These wraps incorporate duck meat and skin, Jasmine Rice, Ginger Slaw, and Hoisin sauce all rolled up in a flour tortilla. Although this wrap uses duck, feel free to substitute roasted chicken in the recipe.

A 4-TO 5-POUND WHOLE DUCKLING, DEFROSTED

1 TABLESPOON SALT

2 TABLESPOONS SHERRY WINE

1 TABLESPOON SOY SAUCE

¼ CUP HONEY

1 TEASPOON GRATED GINGERROOT

Preheat the oven to 400°F. Wash the duck under cold running water, and pat dry with paper towels. Remove any thick pockets of fat and discard. Rub the inside of the duck with the salt. In a small bowl, combine the sherry, soy sauce, honey, and gingerroot. Prick the skin of the duck and brush it with the sauce. Refrigerate the duck for 1 hour. Brush the duck with the sauce again, and place it on a rack in a roasting pan, breast-side up. Bake for 30 minutes, then brush with additional sauce. Turn the duck over and bake for 20 minutes. Turn again and apply more sauce. Bake for an additional 15 minutes, or until the duck is crisp and golden-brown. Remove from the oven, and let cool for 20 minutes. Carve the duck, preserving as much skin as possible, removing all the meat from the bones.

Jasmine Rice

Jasmine Rice is sold in the rice section or Asian foods section of the grocery store. If you cannot find it, substitute Japanese-style short-grain rice.

3 CUPS WATER

3 CUPS JASMINE RICE

Wash the rice well. Drain and place the rice into a 3-quart saucepan with water. Cover and cook on high heat until the water boils. Reduce the heat to medium-low and cook for 10 minutes. Turn off the heat and leave the pot on the stove for another 10 minutes. Stir the cooked rice to make it fluffy.

Ginger Slaw

4 CUPS THINLY SLICED GREEN CABBAGE	1 TEASPOON GRATED FRESH GINGERROOT
1 CUP GRATED CARROT (ABOUT 3 MEDIUM CARROTS)	1 TABLESPOON SUGAR
	2 TABLESPOONS CHOPPED FRESH CILANTRO (OPTIONAL)
4 SCALLIONS (GREEN ONIONS), CHOPPED	
1/2 CUP VEGETABLE OIL	1/2 CUP CHOPPED PEANUTS FOR GARNISH
1/4 CUP RICE WINE VINEGAR	

Combine the cabbage, carrot, and scallions in a large serving bowl. In a small bowl, whisk together the remaining ingredients and pour dressing over the cabbage mixture. Toss to combine and garnish with chopped peanuts. Refrigerate until ready to use.

ASSEMBLY

6 LARGE FLOUR TORTILLAS, WARMED	3 CUPS JASMINE RICE
1 CUP HOISIN SAUCE	5 CUPS GINGER SLAW
4 CUPS COOKED PEKING DUCK, OR ROASTED CHICKEN	CUCUMBER STICKS AND SCALLION FANS FOR GARNISH

Place 1 tortilla onto a serving plate. Spread a layer of Hoisin sauce over the center of the tortilla. Place some of the duck meat, skin down, in the center of the tortilla, then cover with Jasmine Rice and Ginger Slaw. Beginning at the bottom, fold the tortilla up over the filling. Fold in the two sides, and then roll the bottom over the filling, to complete the package. Continue until all the tortillas are wrapped. Serve the wraps garnished with cucumber sticks and scallion fans.

Pesto Swordfish Wraps

Here is an amazing pairing of pesto and swordfish, wrapped in phyllo, and baked in the oven till golden. When these packets are cut open, there is a beautiful contrast between golden-brown pastry and brilliant green sauce against white-fleshed fish. These wraps will become a favorite with your guests. You may substitute sea bass or any other firm, white-fleshed fish.

3 POUNDS 1-INCH-THICK SWORDFISH FILLETS, SKIN AND ANY FATTY SECTIONS REMOVED

½ CUP PREPARED BASIL PESTO (SEE RECIPE, PAGE 124)

2 TABLESPOONS HEAVY CREAM

1 TABLESPOON BALSAMIC VINEGAR

½ POUND PHYLLO DOUGH, DEFROSTED

1 CUP (2 STICKS) MELTED BUTTER, AT ROOM TEMPERATURE

½ CUP DRY BREAD CRUMBS

Cut each swordfish fillet in half. In a small bowl or measuring cup, combine the Basil Pesto with the heavy cream and vinegar. Cover the phyllo with a kitchen towel, and set 1 sheet on a flat surface. Brush the phyllo all over with melted butter, and sprinkle with the bread crumbs. Top with another sheet of phyllo, and brush the top sheet with butter. Sprinkle with bread crumbs. Place the fillet at the top center of the narrow part of the phyllo, leaving about 2 inches at the top. Cover the fillet with 2 tablespoons of the pesto mixture. Fold the top of the phyllo over the fillet, then fold in the sides. Brush the sides with butter, and roll the phyllo up into a package, brushing the packet with butter to seal. Continue until all wraps are assembled. Place the finished packages, pesto-side up, onto a jelly-roll pan that has been lined with parchment or foil. Repeat with the remaining fillets. Refrigerate for up to 8 hours. When ready to bake, preheat the oven to 400°F. Bake the wraps for 25 minutes, or until the pastry is golden-brown. Remove from the oven and serve.

Another way to present the swordfish is to place the fillet at the top of the phyllo and roll it without tucking in the sides. Tie each end with fresh chives, brush with butter, and bake as directed.

Fresh basil is fragile and keeps only a short period of time in the refrigerator. Store it as you would salad greens, but if you cannot use it at its peak, pack it into a 2-cup glass jar, cover it with olive oil (not extra-virgin) and refrigerate. When you need to use fresh basil in a recipe, remove the basil from the oil, and add it to the dish. The oil also takes on the flavor of the basil and you can use it in salad dressings, or to brush on foccaccia bread.

Basil Pesto

MAKES 3 CUPS

Pesto freezes really well, so when basil is plentiful in the summer, make a batch in the food processor for use later in the year.

2 CUPS TIGHTLY PACKED BASIL LEAVES

1 CUP FRESHLY GRATED PARMESAN CHEESE

3 GARLIC CLOVES, PEELED

$^1/_4$ CUP PINE NUTS (PIGNOLI)

$^1/_2$ CUP OLIVE OIL

$^1/_4$ CUP VEGETABLE OIL

In the blender or a food processor, process the basil, cheese, garlic, and pine nuts. With the machine running, gradually add the oils and process until smooth. Pour into a glass jar, and pour $^1/_2$-inch olive oil on the top to seal the Basil Pesto. When ready to use, drain off the oil and stir the pesto. You can also freeze the pesto in zipper-type storage bags or in plastic containers. Defrost the pesto overnight in the refrigerator.

Pilgrim Dinner Wraps

SERVES 6

What to do with all that leftover turkey and dressing from holiday meals? Make dinner wraps! My friend Judy owns a turkey farm in New Hampshire and gave me this idea when she told me she sells out of these at the Portsmouth Farmer's Market every weekend.

2 SHEETS LAVOSH

1/4 CUP MAYONNAISE (OPTIONAL)

12 LETTUCE LEAVES (I LIKE TO USE RED OR GREEN LEAFY LETTUCE)

12 SLICES OF COOKED TURKEY BREAST, OR ABOUT 3 CUPS CHOPPED COOKED TURKEY

2 CUPS LEFTOVER STUFFING (OR FRESHLY MADE)

1 CUP CRANBERRY CHUTNEY (SEE RECIPE, PAGE 126)

1/2 CUP COOKED BACON, CRUMBLED (OPTIONAL)

ADDITIONAL CRANBERRY CHUTNEY FOR GARNISH

PARSLEY BOUQUETS FOR GARNISH

Lay the lavosh on a flat surface or cutting board. Spread a thin layer of mayonnaise over the Lavosh. Beginning with the lettuce, layer the ingredients evenly. Roll each sheet from the long side, and refrigerate in plastic wrap for 2 hours. Remove from the refrigerator and slice into 2-inch slices. Serve garnished with additional Cranberry Chutney and parsley bouquets.

Cranberry Chutney

The unique blending of onions, cranberries, peaches, and pecans seems odd, but the finished product will have you screaming for more. The chutney holds its own in the Pilgrim Wraps, but can also be used alongside the cranberry sauce at holiday time, or served with chicken or pork.

1 CAN (16-OUNCE) PEACH HALVES, PACKED IN SYRUP

1 PACKAGE (12-OUNCE) FRESH OR FROZEN CRANBERRIES

1 1/2 CUPS SUGAR

1 MEDIUM ONION, CHOPPED

1 CUP PECAN HALVES

1/2 TEASPOON GROUND CINNAMON

1/4 CUP DRY GINGER

Drain the peaches, chop coarsely, and reserve the juice. Place cranberries, juice, sugar, and onion in a saucepan over medium-high heat and cook until cranberries begin to "pop." Add pecans, cinnamon, ginger, and peaches and cook for 10 more minutes. Remove from the heat and allow to cool. Pack into 4 two-cup sterilized jars. Refrigerate for up to 2 months.

Pizza Wraps

SERVES 6

Our love affair with pizza knows no bounds; whether it is the traditional Italian-style pie or a designer pizza, there is something special about topping pizza dough with our favorite ingredients. Pizza wraps make a great tool for entertaining. Give each guest their own dough, and then provide various toppings for the pizzas. Have each guest top their pizza dough, then fold, and bake. Identification of their masterpiece can be done by etching initials on top of the dough, or laying fresh herbs in a pattern over the top. Pizza wraps can be frozen after baking, then reheated in a 375°F oven for 20 minutes.

3 TEASPOONS ACTIVE DRY YEAST

2 TEASPOONS SUGAR

2 CUPS WARM WATER (100 TO 110°F)

5 1/2 CUPS ALL-PURPOSE FLOUR

2 TABLESPOONS OLIVE OIL

1 1/2 TEASPOONS SALT

1/2 CUP FRESHLY GRATED PARMESAN CHEESE

In a 4-cup measuring cup, combine the yeast, sugar, and water. Let stand until foamy. Place the remaining ingredients in the food processor, and, with the motor running, pour in the yeast mixture. Process until the dough forms a ball. Turn into a greased bowl, let rise until doubled in bulk (1 hour). Roll the dough into six 10-inch circles. Let rest for 5 to 7 minutes (see Assembly, next page).

Traditional Pizza Sauce

1 LARGE ONION, CHOPPED

2 CLOVES GARLIC, MINCED

2 TABLESPOONS OLIVE OIL

2 CANS (28 OUNCES EACH) CRUSHED
TOMATOES

$^1/_4$ CUP CHOPPED FRESH PARSLEY

1 TEASPOON DRIED BASIL

1 TEASPOON SALT

$^1/_4$ TEASPOON FRESHLY GROUND BLACK
PEPPER

1 TABLESPOON SUGAR

In a medium saucepan, sauté the onion and garlic in the oil until they are translucent. Add the remaining ingredients and allow the sauce to cook down for about 30 minutes, stirring frequently. At this point you can refrigerate the sauce until you are ready to use it (up to 5 days), or freeze it for up to 2 months.

ASSEMBLY

OLIVE OIL FOR GREASING COOKIE SHEETS

PIZZA DOUGH

6 CUPS TRADITIONAL PIZZA SAUCE

2 CUPS GRATED MELTING CHEESE (I LIKE TO
USE AN ASSORTMENT, SUCH AS 1 CUP
GRATED MUENSTER, $^1/_2$ CUP FRESHLY
GRATED PARMESAN, AND $^1/_2$ CUP GRATED
MONTEREY JACK)

2 TABLESPOONS DRIED OREGANO

2 TABLESPOONS OLIVE OIL

ASSORTED TOPPINGS IF DESIRED

Lightly brush cookie sheets with olive oil, and lay the dough into the pans. Spread a layer of Pizza Sauce over half the dough, leaving a 1-inch border around the outside. Sprinkle half the dough with the cheeses, and top with sprinkles of dried oregano and a drizzle of olive oil. Fold the dough over the cheese and seal, brushing with additional olive oil. Bake at 425°F for 20 minutes, or until the crust is golden.

Let your imagination be your guide with toppers for these Pizza Wraps. You can use pepperoni, Italian sausage, veggies, seafood, or any other toppings that are your favorites.

Quesadilla Mercedes

A simple quesadilla is transformed into an elegant entrée with the addition of shrimp to a wonderful ranchero sauce. Although I prefer to bake the quesdillas to give them a crispy texture, you can also microwave them to melt the cheese.

2 TABLESPOONS VEGETABLE OIL

1 LARGE ONION, THINLY SLICED

1 SEEDED GREEN PEPPER, THINLY SLICED

1 SEEDED RED PEPPER, THINLY SLICED

1 TEASPOON CUMIN

4 CUPS TOMATO PUREE

2 TABLESPOONS TEQUILA

SALT AND PEPPER, TO TASTE

1 POUND LARGE SHRIMP, PEELED AND DEVEINED

4 LARGE TORTILLAS

4 CUPS MONTEREY JACK CHEESE

In a 12-inch sauté pan, heat the oil, then add the onion, peppers, and cumin. Cook over medium-high heat, until they are soft. Add the tomatoes and tequila, bringing the mixture to a boil. Simmer for 30 minutes, stirring occasionally. Taste the sauce and season with salt and pepper. When ready to serve, add the shrimp to the sauce, and cook for 2 minutes. Remove from the heat, and stir until the shrimp have turned pink. *Do not overcook,* or the shrimp will be tough. Place the 4 tortillas on 2 cookie sheets. Sprinkle each one with Monterey Jack cheese. Bake in a preheated 375°F oven for 15 minutes, or until the cheese is melted. Remove from the oven. Fold the tortillas in half, and place on dinner plates. Cover the tortillas with the shrimp ranchero sauce. Serve immediately.

Ratatouille Crêpes

Ratatouille, that French mélange of vegetables, becomes a super-star when wrapped in crêpes, and then covered in melted Swiss cheese. The ingredients in the classic ratatouille are included here, but I urge you to use your imagination, and your leftovers, to create wonderful crêpes. If you have leftover steak, chicken, or fish, add them. Crêpes and filling can be prepared and filled up to 2 days ahead of time, requiring just 30 minutes of baking before serving.

12 CRÊPES (SEE RECIPE, PAGE 132)

1 LARGE EGGPLANT

4 MEDIUM ZUCCHINI

2 GREEN PEPPERS

1 RED PEPPER

2 CUPS SLICED ONION (2 LARGE)

4 GARLIC CLOVES, MINCED

$^1/_4$ CUP OLIVE OIL

1 TEASPOON THYME

$^1/_2$ TEASPOON OREGANO

$^1/_2$ TEASPOON ROSEMARY

1 CAN (16-OUNCE) CHOPPED TOMATOES IN JUICE

1 TEASPOON SALT AND $^1/_2$ TEASPOON FRESHLY GROUND PEPPER TO TASTE

1 TABLESPOON SUGAR

NON-STICK VEGETABLE SPRAY

2 CUPS GRATED IMPORTED SWISS CHEESE

Cut the ends off of the eggplant. Dice the eggplant into $^1/_2$-inch pieces. Set aside. Scrub the zucchini, then trim the ends. Cut the zucchini into $^1/_2$-inch rounds. Slice the peppers into thin strips. Heat the olive oil in a 12-inch skillet. Add the peppers, onions, garlic, and herbs to the oil, sautéing over medium-high heat for 10 minutes. Add the eggplant and zucchini, tossing to incorporate with the other vegetables. Add the tomatoes, salt, pepper, and sugar, bringing the mixture to a boil. Cook over high heat for 5 minutes, until the liquid begins to evaporate. Taste the ratatouille for seasoning, and add additional herbs, salt, and pepper, if needed. Set the mixture aside, and cool to room temperature, or refrigerate until ready to use.

Spray a 13 × 9-inch pan with non-stick vegetable spray. Lay 1 crêpe on a flat work surface and spoon some of the ratatouille down the center of the crêpe. Fold both sides over the filling. Lift the crêpe into the pan and place it seam-side down, and continue to prepare the crêpes until the pan is filled. Sprinkle the grated cheese over the top of the crêpes, and bake in a preheated 350°F oven for 30 minutes, or until the cheese is golden. Serve immediately. Leftover ratatouille is delicious in omlettes or tucked into a pita.

To roast peppers: Preheat the broiler for 5 minutes. Place the peppers onto a foil-lined baking pan, and broil 4 inches away from the heat source, turning when the peppers become blackened on all sides. When the peppers have become uniformly roasted, turn off the broiler, close the door to the oven, and let the peppers cool in the oven. The moisture from the peppers will allow the skin to steam, and the peppers will separate easily from the skin. Skin and seed the peppers, and make a dressing from $1/2$ cup of olive oil and $1/3$ cup Balsamic vinegar. Add 3 garlic cloves, sliced in half, plus salt and freshly ground pepper to taste. This salad keeps for 2 weeks in the refrigerator, and is wonderful on crusty bread, as well as an addition to pizzas and calzone. Remove the garlic cloves before serving.

Entrée Crêpes

MAKES 10 TO 12 LARGE CRÊPES

$3/4$ CUP MILK	$1 1/2$ CUPS FLOUR
3 LARGE EGGS	6 TABLESPOONS MELTED BUTTER
$1/4$ TEASPOON SALT	NON-STICK COOKING SPRAY

In a glass mixing bowl, whisk together the milk, eggs, and salt. Gradually add the flour, $1/2$ cup at a time. When the mixture is smooth, whisk in the butter. Refrigerate the crêpe batter for at least one hour, or overnight.

Spray a non-stick 8-inch omelette pan or skillet with non-stick cooking spray. Heat the pan over high heat, and pour in $1/3$ cup of the crêpe batter, or enough to thinly coat the bottom of the pan. (Pour out any excess batter, or the crêpes will be too thick). Cook the crêpe until the underside is lightly browned. Using a spatula, flip the crêpe over and cook for another 30 seconds. Transfer the crêpes to a plate, and continue making the crêpes until the batter is used up. Crêpes may be stored in airtight storage bags for 2 days in the refrigerator, or frozen for up to one month. Defrost overnight in the refrigerator before using.

Rocky Balboa Calzone

All the ingredients of a classic Italian hero sandwich rolled up into a hot package are well worth the caloric splurge. Serve this one while watching a football game on TV—the game will be secondary to your dramatic calzone. A combination of pizza dough folded over savory ingredients, baked in a hot oven, and then cut into while still warm, calzones are a delight to the eye and the palate. There are endless possibilities for stuffing this simple and delicious dough, so try and experiment with your favorites.

The dough is easily put together in the food processor or bread machine, and you can refrigerate or freeze it until you are ready to use it. I like to roll out the dough into a large freeform circle, layering the ingredients on half of the dough, then folding the dough over the filling to produce a huge turnover. The calzone is best eaten the day it is made, but can be baked, and then frozen. Reheat the calzone in a preheated 350°F oven for 30 minutes.

DOUGH

2¹/₂ TEASPOONS ACTIVE DRY YEAST

1¹/₄ CUPS WARM WATER (NOT MORE THAN 110°F)

¹/₄ TEASPOON SUGAR

3 TABLESPOONS OLIVE OIL

3¹/₄ CUPS ALL-PURPOSE FLOUR

2 TEASPOONS SALT

In a measuring cup, combine the water, yeast, and sugar, and stir. Set the mixture aside, until it begins to bubble. (If the yeast does not begin to bubble, discard it and start over.) In the work bowl of a food processor, combine the flour and salt. With the machine running, pour in the yeast mixture, and the oil. Allow the machine to run until a ball of dough forms. (If the dough does not form a ball, add additional flour through the feed tube 2 tablespoons at a time.) Stop the machine, and transfer the dough to a floured board, and knead it about 20 times. Place the dough in an oiled bowl, and let it rise for 1¹/₂ hours, or until doubled in bulk. Punch the dough down, and divide it into two equal parts. Roll out each piece into a 16-to-18-inch circle. Prepare the fillings.

Alternate Method

Have a bread machine? Place all the dough ingredients into the bread machine, and program for "manual" or "dough" setting. Proceed as directed.

FILLING AND ASSEMBLY

OIL FOR BRUSHING COOKIE SHEET

1 TEASPOON DRIED BASIL

1 1/2 TEASPOONS DRIED OREGANO

1/4 CUP OLIVE OIL

1/4 POUND THINLY SLICED GENOA SALAMI (OR PEPPERONI)

1/4 POUND THINLY SLICED MORTADELLA

1/4 POUND THINLY SLICED HOT CAPPACO-LA HAM

5 PEPPERONCINI, STEMS REMOVED AND CHOPPED COARSELY

1/2 CUP SLICED RED ONION

1 ROMA TOMATO, THINLY SLICED AND PAT-TED DRY WITH A PAPER TOWEL

1/2 CUP ROASTED RED PEPPER STRIPS (JARRED OR FRESHLY ROASTED)

1 CUP GRATED PROVOLONE CHEESE, OR SLICED PROVOLONE, TORN INTO PIECES

SESAME OR POPPY SEEDS (OPTIONAL)

Preheat the oven to 375°F. Line a cookie sheet with foil or parchment paper and brush with oil. Place the rolled dough onto the cookie sheet. In a small bowl, combine the basil, oregano, and olive oil. Brush some of the mixture over the surface of the dough. Layer the remaining ingredients over half the dough, leaving an inch free all the way around. Sprinkle 2 tablespoons of the remaining oil over the filling. Fold the dough over and crimp the edges together. Brush the top with the remaining oil, and sprinkle with sesame or poppy seeds, if desired. Repeat with the remaining dough. Bake the calzone for 25 minutes, or until the dough is golden-brown. Remove from the oven, and cool for 10 minutes before cutting and serving.

Roti

*Roti are delicious flatbread-wrapped curry creations that are pop-
ular in the leeward islands of the Caribbean. Found on many
street corner food carts, roti are a great "take-away" lunch, or can
be served as the main course for dinner. Traditional fillings for
roti are curried vegetables, seafood, or chicken. The flatbread is
best eaten the day you cook it, but the dough can be made the day
ahead and cooked about one hour before serving. The fillings can
be prepared two days ahead and refrigerated until ready to serve.
As an alternative to making your own flatbread, you can buy
Indian chappati or paratha breads in Indian and health food
grocery stores.*

Roti Flatbread

2 CUPS ALL-PURPOSE FLOUR

1 TEASPOON BAKING POWDER

1/2 TEASPOON SALT

2 TABLESPOONS PLAIN NONFAT YOGURT

2 TABLESPOONS VEGETABLE OIL

1/2 TO 3/4 CUP WATER

ADDITIONAL VEGETABLE OIL FOR GRILLING

Combine the dry ingredients in a mixing bowl, and stir to blend. Gradually add the
yogurt and oil, stirring with a fork until the mixture begins to come together. Using 2
tablespoons of water at a time, continue to add water, until the dough forms a ball.
Turn the dough out onto a floured board and knead for 5 minutes. When the dough is
elastic, set it aside in a greased bowl for 15 minutes to rest, or refrigerate it for up to
24 hours. Divide the dough into 6 equal-sized balls. Flatten each ball, and roll out on a
floured board into 8-inch circles. Dust the dough with flour and stack on a plate until
ready to cook. When you are ready to serve the Roti, brush a griddle or 10-inch skillet
with a small amount of oil, and heat the griddle over moderately high heat. Place one

dough circle onto the griddle and cook until it is lightly browned on one side. Small bubbles may appear on top of the bread. Turn the bread and cook for an additional minute, brushing the top side with some oil. Remove from the griddle, place on a serving plate, and cover with a clean kitchen towel. Continue cooking the flatbread until all the circles are done.

Curried Chicken and Chick-pea Filling

2 TABLESPOONS BUTTER

2 CLOVES GARLIC, MINCED

1/2 CUP FINELY CHOPPED ONION

1/2 CUP FINELY CHOPPED CARROT

1 TABLESPOON TOMATO PASTE

1 TABLESPOON CURRY POWDER

1/2 CUP CHICKEN BROTH

15 1/2-OUNCE CAN CHICK-PEAS, DRAINED AND RINSED

2 CUPS COOKED CHICKEN, CUT INTO 1/2-INCH PIECES

In a 3-quart saucepan, melt the butter and add the garlic, onion, and carrot, sautéing until the onion begins to become translucent. Add the tomato paste and curry powder, and continue to cook for 2 minutes. Gradually add the chicken broth and chick-peas. Stir the mixture, bringing up any browned bits on the bottom of the pan. Add the chicken and simmer the mixture uncovered for 15 minutes, stirring frequently. Remove the mixture from the heat, and serve immediately, or refrigerate overnight.

Spinach and Potato Filling

This filling is so delicious, you may just want to make it as a side dish for grilled meat or chicken. It keeps for 2 days in the refrigerator.

2 TABLESPOONS VEGETABLE OIL

$^1/_2$ CUP CHOPPED ONION

3 CLOVES GARLIC, MINCED

2 POUNDS FRESH SPINACH, WASHED, AND TOUGH STEMS TRIMMED

1 CUP CHICKEN BROTH

1 TEASPOON CURRY POWDER (ADD MORE IF YOU LIKE YOURS SPICIER)

2 CUPS YUKON GOLD POTATOES, WASHED AND DICED INTO $^1/_2$ INCH PIECES

$^1/_2$ TEASPOON SALT

$^1/_8$ TEASPOONS FRESHLY GROUND BLACK PEPPER

Heat the vegetable oil in a 12-inch sauté pan or wok. Add the onion and garlic, sautéing until the onion becomes translucent. Add the spinach, tossing to coat with the oil. Add the chicken broth, curry powder, and potatoes. Cover the skillet, and cook over medium heat for 20 minutes, stirring a few times during the cooking. Uncover the skillet, taste the spinach for seasoning, and add additional salt and pepper, if necessary. You may serve the filling immediately, or refrigerate it for up to 2 days.

ASSEMBLY

ROTI FLATBREAD

FILLINGS

CUCUMBER YOGURT SAUCE (PAGE 111)

Reheat the fillings, and have the warmed flatbread ready. Place 2 to 3 tablespoons of filling in the center of each flatbread. Fold over the bottom and sides of bread, enclosing the filling as you would a letter in an envelope. Serve 2 roti per person, and pass Cucumber Yogurt Sauce separately.

Salmon Pitas

SERVES 6

Salmon cakes, wrapped in pita and covered with Lemon Dill Mayonnaise, make a great dinner, especially when you are trying to recycle leftover salmon. The salmon cakes can be prepared the day before, and the mayonnaise keeps in the refrigerator for about a week. This recipe works well with any cooked fish, shellfish, or even chicken.

2 CUPS COOKED SALMON, BONES REMOVED, FLAKED

2 TABLESPOONS CHOPPED ONION

1 CUP SOFT BREAD CRUMBS

1 TABLESPOON MAYONNAISE

1 TABLESPOON WORCESTERSHIRE SAUCE

$\frac{1}{2}$ TEASPOON SALT

1 TABLESPOON CAPERS, DRAINED

1 TEASPOON DRY MUSTARD

1 EGG, BEATEN

1 CUP DRY BREAD CRUMBS

2 TABLESPOONS BUTTER

2 TABLESPOONS VEGETABLE OIL

6 PITAS

LEMON DILL MAYONNAISE (RECIPE ON NEXT PAGE)

DRAINED CAPERS FOR GARNISH

CHOPPED FRESH PARSLEY FOR GARNISH

Combine the salmon, onion, soft bread crumbs, mayonnaise, Worcestershire, salt, capers, mustard, and egg in a mixing bowl. Shape the salmon mixture into 2-inch patties. Dip the patties into the dry bread crumbs and refrigerate for at least 1 hour. Melt the butter in the oil over medium-high heat. Add the salmon patties, turning when they become golden on one side. Remove the salmon cakes to paper towels and drain. Lay each pita on a flat surface and place two salmon cakes in the center. Top with 2 tablespoons of the Lemon Dill Mayonnaise (recipe on next page), and garnish with additional capers and chopped parsley. Roll up the pitas and secure with toothpicks, or use long strips of green onion or chives to tie each wrap.

Lemon Dill Mayonnaise

1½ CUPS PREPARED MAYONNAISE

2 TEASPOONS LEMON JUICE

1 TEASPOON LEMON ZEST

2 TABLESPOONS FINELY CHOPPED RED ONION

1 TEASPOON WORCESTERSHIRE SAUCE

3 TABLESPOONS CHOPPED FRESH DILL

1 TABLESPOON CHOPPED FRESH PARSLEY

SALT AND FRESHLY GROUND BLACK PEPPER TO TASTE (OPTIONAL)

Combine all the ingredients in a small mixing bowl. Taste for seasoning and add additional dill, and salt and pepper if desired.

Sausage and Pepper Wraps

SERVES 6

A distant cousin to the Philly cheesesteak, these are found on boardwalks up and down the East Coast. Traditionally, a French roll is stuffed with Italian sausages, then covered with peppers and onions in a tomato sauce. We'll roll ours in pita bread, cut turkey sausage into rounds, and sauté it with the peppers, giving us a lighter and more flavorful version of the original.

1 TABLESPOON OLIVE OIL

8 LINKS OF ITALIAN TURKEY SAUSAGE, CUT INTO 1-INCH ROUNDS

1 LARGE ONION, THINLY SLICED

1 RED PEPPER, THINLY SLICED

1 GREEN PEPPER, THINLY SLICED

1 CAN (16-OUNCE) CHOPPED TOMATOES, DRAINED

1 TEASPOON SALT

1/2 TEASPOON FRESHLY GROUND BLACK PEPPER

1 TEASPOON DRIED OREGANO

1/2 TEASPOON DRIED BASIL

6 PITAS

1 CUP GRATED MOZZARELLA CHEESE (OPTIONAL)

Heat the oil in a 12-inch sauté pan or wok. Add the turkey sausage, tossing to brown evenly. Add the onion and red and green peppers, sautéing until the vegetables have softened. Add the tomatoes and the seasonings, bringing the mixture to a boil, then simmer for 15 minutes. The sausage mixture can be refrigerated for up to 3 days before serving. Cut each pita in half, fill the pocket with some of the sausage mixture, and the optional cheese if you are using it. Serve immediately.

Seafood Lasagna Wraps

SERVES 6 TO 8

An elegant dinner for family or friends, this beautiful combination of delicate seafood, creamy white sauce, and chunky tomato sauce makes a dramatic presentation. A wonderful do-ahead dish, the components and the completed dish can be refrigerated for 2 days, or frozen for 1 month. Spinach lasagna noodles give this dish a special look, but if you would prefer to use plain lasagna noodles, feel free to substitute. For another twist on this wrap, substitute 4 cups cooked salmon for the shellfish and make the sauce without the cooking liquid, thinning with a little fish stock, or heavy cream.

1 POUND SPINACH LASAGNA NOODLES, COOKED AND DRAINED

2 POUNDS SHELLFISH (ANY COMBINATION OF SHRIMP, SCALLOPS, CRAB, AND LOBSTER, PEELED AND DEVEINED, SHELLS REMOVED)

$1/4$ CUP ($1/2$ STICK) PLUS 2 TABLESPOONS BUTTER

2 TABLESPOONS WHITE WINE

2 CUPS RICOTTA CHEESE

$1/4$ CUP CHOPPED FRESH PARSLEY

$1/2$ CUP GRATED PARMESAN CHEESE

THE RESERVED COOKING LIQUID

$1/4$ CUP ALL-PURPOSE FLOUR

$1\,1/2$ CUPS MILK

$1/8$ TEASPOON WHITE PEPPER

DASH OF NUTMEG

$1/3$ CUP HEAVY CREAM

4 CUPS TOMATO SAUCE (SEE RECIPE, PAGE 103)

ADDITIONAL GRATED PARMESAN CHEESE

In a 12-inch sauté pan, melt 2 tablespoons of the butter and add the seafood. Sauté until the shrimp begin to turn pink and the scallops are opaque. Add the wine and cook for an additional minute. Drain the seafood, reserving the liquid. In a large mixing bowl, combine the ricotta with the seafood and parsley. Add 2 tablespoons of the reserved cooking liquid and the Parmesan cheese. Refrigerate until ready to roll the noodles. In a 3-quart saucepan, melt the butter and add the flour, cooking until smooth. Gradually pour in the milk and the remaining cooking liquid, whisking until smooth. Add the white pepper, nutmeg, heavy cream, and cook until the mixture is thickened. Set aside.

Spread 1 cup of the Tomato Sauce over the bottom of a 13 × 9-inch ovenproof baking dish. Working with the cooled lasagna noodles, spread some of the seafood ricotta mixture over a lasagna noodle, roll up the noodle, and place it seam-side down in the prepared casserole dish. Cover each wrap with some of the cream sauce, and finish each one with some of the Tomato Sauce. Sprinkle with additional grated Parmesan cheese. Bake, covered with aluminum foil, in a 350°F oven for 30 minutes. Remove the foil, and bake for an additional 20 minutes.

To store Parmesan cheese so that it won't harden into a rock-solid block, pour 2 tablespoons of olive oil onto a paper towel. Cover the cheese in the paper towel, store in an airtight plastic bag, and refrigerate. This should keep the cheese pliable for grating for up to 2 months.

Sesame Chicken Wraps

SERVES 6

Succulent chicken is marinated in a soy and sesame oil sauce, then quickly grilled, and tucked into flour tortillas with rice and a sweet hot pineapple salsa, for a Pacific rim taste that is out of this world.

Cooked Sesame Chicken

4 WHOLE BONELESS, SKINLESS CHICKEN BREASTS

2 TABLESPOONS SUGAR

2 TABLESPOONS RICE WINE OR SHERRY

$^1/_2$ CUP SOY SAUCE

2 TABLESPOONS SESAME OIL

$^1/_4$ CUP SESAME SEEDS

Cut each chicken breast into 4 or 5 strips about $^1/_2$ to $^3/_4$ inches wide. Place them in a zipper-type storage bag. In a small mixing bowl, blend together the remaining ingredients. Pour the marinade over the chicken and marinate for 2 hours or overnight. When ready to serve, preheat the grill or broiler, and broil for 3 to 4 minutes on each side, or until the chicken is done.

Pineapple Salsa

$1^1/_2$ CUPS CHOPPED FRESH PINEAPPLE

$^1/_4$ CUP CHOPPED ANAHEIM CHILI PEPPERS, SEEDED

1 TABLESPOON CHOPPED FRESH CILANTRO

2 TABLESPOONS SUGAR

$^1/_4$ CUP RICE VINEGAR

1 TABLESPOON LIME JUICE

$^1/_4$ CUP CHOPPED RED ONION

In a small glass bowl, combine the pineapple, chili pepper, and cilantro. Set aside. Combine the sugar, rice vinegar, and lime juice in a saucepan. Bring to a boil, and stir until the sugar dissolves. Pour over the pineapple mixture, stirring to blend. Add the red onion, and chill the mixture until ready to serve. The salsa will keep in the refrigerator for about 3 days.

ASSEMBLY

6 FLOUR TORTILLAS	PINEAPPLE SALSA
JASMINE RICE (SEE RECIPE, PAGE 120)	FRESH PINEAPPLE SPEARS FOR GARNISH
COOKED SESAME CHICKEN	FRESH CILANTRO SPRIGS FOR GARNISH

Place 1 tortilla on a flat surface, and lay about $^1/_3$ cup of rice down the center of the tortilla. Top the rice with 3 or 4 pieces of chicken, and $^1/_4$ cup of the Pineapple Salsa. Roll the bottom of the tortilla up over the filling, and fold in the sides. Roll the bottom over the filling to make the package. Prepare the remaining 5 tortillas in the same way. Serve garnished with fresh pineapple spears and sprigs of cilantro.

Sole Wraps

Fillet of sole makes its own wrap, when stuffed with a savory mixture of crab and shrimp, then covered in a delicious sherry sauce. This is the perfect dinner for company. It can be made ahead of time, and requires only 12 minutes of cooking in a hot oven.

5 TABLESPOONS BUTTER	6 PIECES FILLET OF SOLE
1 GARLIC CLOVE, MINCED	$^1/_2$ CUP WHITE WINE
1 CUP FINELY CHOPPED COOKED SHRIMP	3 TABLESPOONS ALL-PURPOSE FLOUR
$^1/_2$ CUP CRABMEAT	2 CUPS MILK
2 CUPS SOFT BREAD CRUMBS	$^1/_4$ CUP SHERRY
$^1/_2$ TEASPOON DRY MUSTARD	$^1/_8$ TEASPOON GRATED NUTMEG
$^1/_2$ CUP MAYONNAISE	WHOLE COOKED SHRIMP OR CRAB CLAWS FOR GARNISH
1 TEASPOON WORCESTERSHIRE SAUCE	

In a small sauté pan, melt 2 tablespoons of the butter, and add the garlic. Sauté until the garlic is soft. Add the shrimp and crab, tossing to coat with the butter. Remove the seafood to a mixing bowl. Add the bread crumbs, mustard, mayonnaise, and Worcestershire sauce. Blend the mixture together and refrigerate until ready to use. Pat the fillets dry, and place 3 to 4 tablespoons of the filling in the center of each, rolling the sole fillets gently. Grease an 11 × 7-inch baking pan, and place the rolls into the pan. Add $^1/_2$ cup white wine, and bake in a preheated 400°F oven for 12 to 17 minutes, or until the fish is done. While the fish is cooking, melt the remaining 3 tablespoons of butter in a 2-quart saucepan. Add the flour, and whisk until the bubbles begin to turn white. Add the milk, sherry, and nutmeg, whisking until the mixture comes to a boil and thickens. (The sauce can be made up to 2 days ahead and refrigerated. Reheat over a low flame before serving.) Place 2 tablespoons of the sauce on the plate, then top with a sole wrap. Cover with additional sauce. Garnish with whole shrimp or crab claws.

Spicy Shrimp and Black Bean Wraps

SERVES 6

Shrimp marinated in spices, then cooked quickly, nestles in a tortilla with black beans and a delicious salad flavored with cilantro, jicama, and oranges. The ingredients can all be assembled ahead of time, with the shrimp getting a last-minute cooking before rolling. This is a perfect 30-minute dinner. If you have leftover chicken or seafood, substitute it for the shrimp.

2 POUNDS LARGE SHRIMP, PEELED AND DEVEINED

1 TABLESPOON CAJUN SEASONING (SEE RECIPE, PAGE 86)

1 CUP VEGETABLE OIL

2 TABLESPOONS FRESH LIME JUICE

1 GARLIC CLOVE, MINCED

1 TEASPOON DRIED OREGANO

2 TABLESPOONS CHOPPED FRESH PARSLEY

1 RECIPE BLACK BEANS OLÉ (SEE RECIPE, PAGE 25)

1 CUP JULIENNED JICAMA

1 CUP ORANGE SECTIONS

$1/2$ CUP CHOPPED FRESH CILANTRO

$1/4$ CUP FRESH LEMON JUICE

2 TABLESPOONS SUGAR

1 TEASPOON SALT

$1/2$ TEASPOON FRESHLY GROUND BLACK PEPPER

4 CUPS SHREDDED LETTUCE

2 TABLESPOONS OLIVE OIL

12 SMALL CORN TORTILLAS

ADDITIONAL CHOPPED FRESH CILANTRO AND ORANGE SECTIONS FOR GARNISH

In a large glass bowl, combine the shrimp, Cajun Seasoning, $1/4$ cup of the vegetable oil, lime juice, garlic, oregano, and parsley. Marinate in the refrigerator for 2 hours, or overnight. (The longer it marinates, the spicier the shrimp.)

Heat the Black Beans Olé to serving temperature and set aside. In a large salad bowl, combine the lettuce, jicama, orange sections, and cilantro. Whisk together the lemon juice, the remaining $3/4$ cup vegetable oil, sugar, salt, and pepper in another bowl. Pour over the lettuce and toss to combine. Remove the shrimp from the refrigerator, drain, and heat the olive oil in a 12-inch sauté pan. When the oil is hot, add the shrimp to the pan and toss until the shrimp are pink. Remove to a heated serving platter. To serve, place a portion of beans into each corn tortilla, top with 3 to 4 shrimp, then the salad, rolling as you would a taco. Serve immediately, garnished with additional cilantro and orange sections.

Steak and Garlic Mashed Potato Wraps

SERVES 6

Elegant and down home all at the same time, these wraps are dressed-up comfort food. Filet mignon is topped with garlic mashed potatoes, then wrapped up in phyllo, set in a luxurious Shiitake Merlot sauce. The mashed potatoes, beef, and sauce can be made two days ahead, and the wraps can be assembled the day before serving and refrigerated.

SALT AND PEPPER TO SEASON

6 FILET MIGNONS (ABOUT 5 OUNCES EACH), CUT 1 INCH THICK

5 TABLESPOONS BUTTER

4 LARGE BAKING POTATOES, PEELED, IF DESIRED, AND CUT INTO $1/2$-INCH CHUNKS

6 GARLIC CLOVES, PEELED

WATER, TO COVER

$1/4$ CUP SOUR CREAM

2 TABLESPOONS GRATED PARMESAN CHEESE

$1/2$ POUND PHYLLO DOUGH

1 CUP (2 STICKS) BUTTER, MELTED AND COOLED

1 CUP DRY BREAD CRUMBS

SHIITAKE MERLOT SAUCE (RECIPE ON NEXT PAGE)

CHOPPED FRESH PARSLEY FOR GARNISH

Season the filets with salt and pepper. Heat 1 tablespoon of the butter in a 12-inch sauté pan, and brown the meat on both sides. Set aside and refrigerate. Place the potatoes and garlic into a 4-quart saucepan, cover with water. Boil the potatoes for 20 minutes, or until they are tender. Drain the potatoes thoroughly, and place in a mixing bowl. Mash the potatoes with the remaining 4 tablespoons butter, sour cream, and cheese, adding additional butter if needed. The potatoes should not be runny. Refrigerate the potatoes. Place the phyllo on a flat work surface and cover with a kitchen towel. Remove 1 piece of phyllo from the stack and brush all over with melted butter. Sprinkle with bread crumbs. Lay another piece of phyllo on top of the first, and brush with melted butter and bread crumbs. Fold the phyllo in half lengthwise, and brush with additional melted butter. Place a filet at the top of the phyllo, leaving a 1-inch border at the top. Top the filet with 2 to 3 tablespoons of potatoes. Fold the top over the filet, fold in the sides, brush with melted butter, then roll the package, sealing with more butter. Place the package, potato-side up, on a jelly-roll pan lined with foil. Continue until all packets are assembled. Refrigerate until ready to bake. When ready to bake, preheat the oven to 400°F, and bake the packets for 20 minutes, or until the phyllo is golden-brown. To serve, ladle 2 to 4 tablespoons Shiitake Merlot Sauce on the dinner plate and center the phyllo packet on top. Garnish with chopped fresh parsley.

Shiitake Merlot Sauce

Merlot has become the darling red wine of the '90s. If you would prefer to use another type of wine, try a Cabernet or Bordeaux.

2 TABLESPOONS BUTTER	1/2 CUP MERLOT
1/2 CUP CHOPPED ONION	1 TEASPOON DRIED THYME
1 CUP SLICED SHIITAKE MUSHROOMS	2 TABLESPOONS VERY COLD BUTTER, CUT INTO 1/2-INCH BITS
1 CUP BEEF BROTH	

In a small saucepan, melt the butter and add the onion and mushrooms, sautéing for 3 minutes. Gradually pour in the beef broth, Merlot, and thyme, bringing the sauce to a boil. Simmer uncovered for 10 minutes. The sauce can be made several days ahead and reheated before serving. Before serving, bring the sauce to a rolling boil, whisking in the cold butter bits a little at a time, until the sauce is glossy and thickened. Serve immediately.

Stuffed Cabbage Rolls

SERVES 6

A reminder of dinner at Mom's, this dish is comfort food at its best. Served on a cold, winter's day with mashed potatoes, this will warm the tummy and the heart. I have reduced the amount of beef from the traditional recipe, to give it a lighter texture.

8 LARGE CABBAGE LEAVES

1/2 POUND GROUND BEEF

1/2 POUND GROUND TURKEY

1/2 CUP FINELY CHOPPED ONION

1/2 CUP COOKED RICE

1/2 CUP KETCHUP

1 TEASPOON SALT

1/2 TEASPOON FRESHLY GROUND BLACK PEPPER

1/2 TEASPOON DRIED THYME

3 CUPS TOMATO PUREE

1 ONION, SLICED (ABOUT 1 CUP)

2 TABLESPOONS WHITE VINEGAR

1/4 CUP SUGAR

Soften the cabbage leaves by placing them in a bowl of very hot water. Remove them, and set aside. In a mixing bowl, combine the beef, turkey, onion, rice, ketchup, salt, pepper, and thyme. Blend the ingredients together, and form the mixture into 8 portions. Place a portion in the center of each cabbage leaf, and roll each cabbage leaf into a packet around the filling. In a 5-quart pan, combine the tomato puree, onion, vinegar, and sugar. Place the rolls, seam-side down, on top of the sauce. Bring the mixture to a boil, reduce to a simmer, and simmer covered for 1 hour. Good served with mashed potatoes.

Tandoori Chicken Wraps

SERVES 6

The Indians have baked in tandoor ovens for centuries. This recipe takes the age-old technique and adapts it to our home kitchens. The chicken turns a coral color when marinated in the spices, then it is wrapped in pita with a cooling cucumber salad. This recipe calls for saffron, which can purchased in most supermarkets. The chicken can be served warm, cold, or at room temperature, so this makes the perfect summer meal.

Tandoori Chicken

1 TEASPOON SAFFRON THREADS, SOAKED IN 3 TABLESPOONS BOILING WATER FOR 5 MINUTES

2 CUPS PLAIN YOGURT

1 TEASPOON SALT

2 TEASPOONS CORIANDER SEEDS, CRUSHED

$^1/_2$ TEASPOON GROUND CUMIN

2 GARLIC CLOVES, MINCED

$^1/_4$ TEASPOON CAYENNE PEPPER

3 WHOLE CHICKEN BREASTS

Combine the saffron and soaking water with the yogurt, salt, coriander, cumin, garlic, and cayenne. Marinate the chicken breasts in this mixture in the refrigerator for at least 24 hours, turning the chicken in the marinade several times before cooking to coat evenly.

Preheat the oven to 400°F. Arrange the chicken pieces side by side on a rack in a shallow roasting pan. Pour any liquid from the marinade over the chicken, and roast for about 15 minutes. Reduce the heat to 350°F and continue roasting for 50 minutes. Remove from the oven, and cut the chicken into 2-inch-wide strips, discarding the bones.

Cucumber Salad

½ **CUP WHITE VINEGAR**

¼ **CUP WATER**

⅓ **CUP SUGAR**

1 HOT HOUSE CUCUMBER, WASHED AND CUT INTO ½-INCH SLICES

4 SCALLIONS (GREEN ONIONS), CHOPPED

1 RED PEPPER, SLICED INTO THIN STRIPS

Combine the vinegar, water, and sugar in a small saucepan, and boil until the sugar is dissolved. Pour over the cucumber, onions, and red pepper. Toss the mixture, and refrigerate for at least 4 hours.

ASSEMBLY

6 PITAS

TANDOORI CHICKEN

2 CUPS CUCUMBER SALAD, DRAINED

Place 1 pita on a flat surface or cutting board. Arrange the chicken down the center of the pita and cover with some of the Cucumber Salad. Roll the pita and secure with toothpicks. Continue until the remaining 5 pitas are assembled. Serve warm, cold, or at room temperature.

Teriyaki Chicken Wraps

Marinated chicken, rolled with Jasmine Rice and stir-fried veggies, makes a wrap that you can put together in less than 40 minutes. The chicken can marinate overnight, or you can use leftover chicken and sauté it in the teriyaki marinade. Use this wrap to recycle any leftover veggies that you might have, such as carrots or broccoli.

½ CUP SOY SAUCE

2 TABLESPOONS VEGETABLE OIL

¼ CUP MIRIN RICE WINE OR SHERRY

2 TABLESPOONS SUGAR

1 TEASPOON GRATED GINGERROOT

4 WHOLE CHICKEN BREASTS, SKINNED AND BONED, CUT LENGTHWISE INTO ½-INCH STRIPS

1 TABLESPOON VEGETABLE OIL

1 ONION, SLICED THINLY

2 CARROTS, CUT INTO 1-INCH MATCHSTICKS

2 CUPS BROCCOLI FLORETS

½ CUP SNOW PEAS, CUT IN HALF ON THE DIAGONAL

6 FLOUR TORTILLAS

1 RECIPE JASMINE RICE (PAGE 120)

FOR GARNISH:

½ CUP CARROT STICKS

4 GREEN ONIONS, CUT INTO 2-INCH PIECES

In a zipper-type storage bag or a shallow glass bowl, combine the soy sauce, oil, rice wine, sugar, and grated ginger. Add the chicken and marinate overnight.

Heat the oil in a wok or 12-inch sauté pan. Drain the chicken and add it to the wok. Stir-fry until the chicken is cooked through. Remove the chicken from the skillet and add the vegetables to the pan, stir-frying until the vegetables are still crisp, but tender. Return the chicken to the wok and keep warm. Place the flour tortillas on serving plates. Spread one-sixth of the Jasmine Rice over the bottom of each tortilla and cover with some of the Teriyaki chicken mixture. Beginning at the bottom of the tortilla, fold the bottom over the filling, then fold in the sides, and roll the bottom over the filling to enclose the package. Complete making the 6 wraps. Serve the chicken wraps garnished with carrot sticks and green onion fans.

Thai Shrimp with Peanut Sauce Wraps

SERVES 6

Thai cuisine incorporates simple ingredients that result in complex flavors. These wraps pair grilled shrimp with a peanut sauce wrapped in lettuce leaves with Ginger Slaw. I have toned down the heat in this wrap, but if you prefer your food extra-hot, add additional hot pepper sauce to the peanut sauce. Try this peanut sauce with pork or chicken, too.

2 TABLESPOONS VEGETABLE OIL

1 GARLIC CLOVE, MINCED

1/2 CUP CHICKEN BROTH

1/4 CUP CREAMY PEANUT BUTTER

1/4 CUP HEAVY CREAM

1 TEASPOON SUGAR

1 TABLESPOON SOY SAUCE

1/4 TEASPOON HOT PEPPER SAUCE

1 TABLESPOON VEGETABLE OIL

1 TABLESPOON SESAME OIL

1/2 TEASPOON MINCED GINGER

1 TEASPOON MINCED GARLIC

2 POUNDS LARGE SHRIMP, PEELED AND DEVEINED

12 WHOLE LETTUCE LEAVES, WASHED AND DRIED

1 RECIPE GINGER SLAW (PAGE 121)

1 RECIPE JASMINE RICE (PAGE 120)

1/2 CUP CHOPPED PEANUTS FOR GARNISH

Heat 1 tablespoon of the vegetable oil in a 2-quart saucepan, then add the minced garlic clove, sautéing for 1 minute. Gradually add the chicken broth, peanut butter, cream, sugar, soy and hot pepper sauces, whisking until smooth and the peanut butter and sugar have dissolved. Remove from the heat until ready to serve.

Heat the remaining tablespoon of vegetable oil and the sesame oil in a wok over medium-high heat. Add the minced ginger and garlic, tossing for 30 seconds. Add the shrimp, and toss the shrimp until they turn pink, about 3 minutes. Remove from the heat and add 1/4 cup of the reserved peanut sauce to the shrimp.

To assemble the wraps, place 3 shrimp into a lettuce leaf, top with 1 tablespoon of peanut sauce and 2 tablespoons of Ginger Slaw. Roll the lettuce leaves around the filling and secure with toothpicks. Serve each person 2 wraps plus some Jasmine Rice, and garnish with chopped peanuts.

Sweet Wraps

JUST DESSERTS

Desserts are the sweet ending to a meal, and these desserts take a little liberty with our term "wrapped." In this chapter I've wrapped chocolate around strawberries, bananas, and pears; crêpes and pancakes are wrapped around sweet fillings; phyllo dough is used to make cheesecake, and cookies as thin as pancakes are baked, then formed and wrapped around a variety of interesting fillings. Dessert wraps can be prepared ahead of time and refrigerated or frozen before using.

Once again, enjoy these wraps, and take stock of their textures, flavors, and contrasts. Where the filling is sweet, use a bland wrapper; or if the filling is bland, use a wrapper that will make a statement. A dessert buffet featuring wraps is the perfect ending to a meal. Place the wraps and a variety of fillings on the buffet counter, then let your guests help themselves. You will be surprised how creative they can be!

Almond Cinnamon Palmiers

Bananas Fosters' Wraps

Berry Turnovers

Cappuccino Wraps

Caramel Apple Wraps

Cheesecake Wraps

Chocolate Cannoli

Cookie Wraps

Cream Puff/Éclair Wraps

Gorilla Wraps

Peach Praline Purses

Poached Pear Wraps

Pumpkin Hazelnut Wraps

Raspberry Napoleon Wraps

Tuxedo-Wrapped Strawberries

Volcanic Hawaiian Wraps

Almond Cinnamon Palmiers

Delicate puff pastry wraps around cinnamon-sugar and almonds to produce a scrumptious, crackly cookie to serve with ice cream or cappuccino. The cookies can be rolled ahead of time and refrigerated for two days or frozen 2 months until you are ready to bake them. You can bake the cookies and store them in zipper-type freezer bags for up to 2 months.

1 17¼ OUNCE PACKAGE FROZEN PUFF PASTRY DOUGH

½ CUP SUGAR

1 TEASPOON GROUND CINNAMON

½ CUP SLIVERED ALMONDS

Preheat the oven to 400°F. Defrost the puff pastry dough according to the manufacturer's directions. Stir the sugar and cinnamon in a small bowl. Using cinnamon-sugar as you would flour, roll out the pastry into a 12 × 18-inch rectangle. Spread the almonds over the pastry, and press them into the dough with your hands. Beginning on one long side, roll the pastry toward the middle, stopping at the middle. Roll the other side in the same manner. Slice off ¼ inch from both ends and discard. Slice the cookies into ³/₄ -inch slices and place on cookie sheets that have been lined with foil or parchment. Sprinkle the cookies with additional cinnamon sugar, if desired, and bake the cookies for 12 to 15 minutes, until they are golden-brown. Remove to wire racks to cool.

Bananas Fosters' Wraps

Bananas become more than that pedestrian partner for corn-flakes when they are married in this cinnamon-scented, decadent sauce of butter, brown sugar, Kahlua, and cream. Wrapped in delicate crepes, this adaptation of a New Orleans favorite is served with vanilla ice cream and shaved chocolate. The crêpes and sauce can be made 2 days ahead of time, and refrigerated until ready to use.

½ CUP (1 STICK) BUTTER

½ CUP BROWN SUGAR

1 TABLESPOON LEMON JUICE

4 RIPE BANANAS, PEELED AND SLICED INTO ½-INCH ROUNDS

½ TEASPOON GROUND CINNAMON

¼ CUP KAHLÚA

½ CUP HEAVY CREAM

12 DESSERT CRÊPES (SEE RECIPE, PAGE 180)

½ CUP GRANULATED SUGAR

1 TEASPOON GROUND CINNAMON

VANILLA ICE CREAM AS ACCOMPANIMENT

SHAVED CHOCOLATE FOR GARNISH

Melt the butter in a 10-inch sauté pan. Add the brown sugar and lemon juice, stirring until the sugar is melted. Add the bananas and cinnamon, stirring to coat the bananas with the sauce. Add the Kahlúa and cream, cooking over medium-low heat until the sauce is thickened. Swirl some of the sauce onto each serving plate. Working with the crêpes on a flat surface, arrange some of the bananas and a bit of sauce down the center of each crêpe. Roll up the crêpes, and center in the sauce, 2 per serving plate. Combine the sugar and cinnamon, and sprinkle a bit over each serving. Serve with a small scoop of vanilla ice cream on the side. Garnish with shaved chocolate.

Berry Turnovers

SERVES 6 TO 8

This wrap combines a flaky pie crust wrapped around fresh berries, then baked to produce a turnover bursting with gorgeous color and taste. The only way to serve these is warm with vanilla ice cream. The pastry can be made ahead and frozen, or the turnovers can be filled and frozen until ready to bake. If you would prefer to use frozen puff pastry sheets for these turnovers, follow the package directions for rolling and baking.

Pastry

2 CUPS ALL-PURPOSE FLOUR	1/3 CUP BUTTER (CUT INTO 1/2-INCH BITS)
2 TABLESPOONS SUGAR	1/3 CUP SOLID VEGETABLE SHORTENING
1 TEASPOON GRATED LEMON ZEST	1/3 CUP COLD WATER

Place the flour, sugar, and lemon zest into a mixing bowl. Using a pastry blender, or two knives, cut the butter and shortening into the flour until it is the size of small peas. Add the water, a tablespoon at a time, until the mixture begins to pull together. When the dough appears to pull together, gather it up into a ball, and flatten. Cut the dough in half and wrap each half in plastic wrap. Refrigerate for 1 hour.

Flour a pastry board and roll out the pastry into an 18-inch circle or rectangle. Cut out 4 four-inch circles. Repeat with the second half of the pastry.

Berry Filling

4 CUPS MIXED BERRIES (I LIKE TO USE
BLACKBERRIES, RASPBERRIES, AND BOY-
SENBERRIES)

1/2 CUP SUGAR

1 TABLESPOON LEMON JUICE

3 TABLESPOONS CORNSTARCH

2 TABLESPOONS BUTTER, CUT INTO BITS

Place the berries in a large mixing bowl. Add the remaining ingredients, and toss well.

ASSEMBLY

8 PASTRY CIRCLES

BERRY FILLING

NON-STICK VEGETABLE SPRAY

1/8 CUP MILK

GRANULATED SUGAR FOR SPRINKLING ON
TURNOVERS

Arrange 1/2 cup berry mixture on one-half of each circle. Fold the circle over and crimp the edges. Make two small slits in the top of the turnover, then transfer turnover to a baking sheet that has been lined with foil and sprayed with non-stick vegetable spray. Continue until all turnovers are assembled. The turnovers can either be baked immediately, held in the refrigerator for up to 4 hours, or frozen before baking. When you are ready to bake the turnovers, preheat the oven to 400°F. Brush the turnovers with milk and sprinkle with granulated sugar. Bake for 20 to 30 minutes, or until the tops are golden. Remove from the oven, and let rest for 15 minutes. Serve warm.

Cappuccino Wraps

SERVES 6 TO 8

Espresso cream, cinnamon, and a little shaved chocolate combine in this extravagant dessert to satisfy the caffeine and chocolate lovers in your house. We'll make chocolate cups flavored with espresso, fill them with cinnamon-scented coffee cream, then garnish with shaved chocolate. The cups and cream can be made up to 2 days ahead and refrigerated. The cups can also be stored in the freezer for 2 months.

8 OUNCES SEMISWEET CHOCOLATE

2 TABLESPOONS STRONG BREWED COFFEE OR ESPRESSO

1 1/2 CUPS MILK

1/2 CUP SUGAR

3 TABLESPOONS ESPRESSO OR STRONGLY BREWED COFFEE

5 EGG YOLKS

1 CUP HEAVY CREAM, STIFFLY WHIPPED

1/4 TEASPOON GROUND CINNAMON

SHAVED CHOCOLATE FOR GARNISH

UNSWEETENED WHIPPED CREAM (OPTIONAL)

Melt the chocolate and coffee in a double boiler or in a microwavable bowl. Prepare molds: either line custard cups with paper liners, or line the inside of shaped containers such as scallop shells or small tea cups with foil. Spread a layer of chocolate over each mold. Allow to sit at room temperature until set, and remove the liner. Store airtight at room temperature for 2 days (if it is hot, refrigerate), or freeze for up to 2 months.

Heat the milk and sugar in a microwavable bowl for 2 minutes at high power. Slowly add the egg yolks to the milk, whisking in as you do. Cook uncovered at 50% power for 6 minutes, stirring every 2 minutes, until the sauce is thick. Add the espresso and refrigerate until cold. When the custard is cooled, fold in the whipped cream and cinnamon. Refrigerate for up to 2 days, whisking before serving. When ready to serve, place 1/3 cup espresso cream into each cup, and garnish with shaved chocolate and also unsweetened whipped cream, if desired.

Caramel Apple Wraps

Another crêpe creation, featuring apples in a caramel sauce, this dish is just as delicious for breakfast as it is for dessert. The apples and sauce can be prepared ahead of time, and refrigerated for 4 days or frozen for two months. Fresh crêpes can be purchased in the produce department of some grocers. See Source Guide, page 183.

1 CUP (2 STICKS) BUTTER

1/2 CUP GRANULATED SUGAR

1/2 CUP BROWN SUGAR

4 CUPS SLICED APPLES (ABOUT 4 LARGE GRANNY SMITHS)

1 CUP HEAVY CREAM

1 TABLESPOON BOURBON

12 DESSERT CRÊPES (PAGE 180)

VANILLA ICE CREAM FOR ACCOMPANIMENT (OPTIONAL)

Melt the butter in a 10-inch sauté pan. Add the sugars, stirring until they are melted. Add the apples, and sauté over medium-high heat until the apples begin to soften, about 4 minutes. Bring the mixture to a boil, and add the heavy cream. Boil the mixture until it is thickened. Add the Bourbon and remove from the heat. Swirl some of the sauce (without the apples) onto each serving plate. Working with the crêpes on a flat work surface, arrange some of the apples on each crêpe, then roll up the crêpes, and set two in the center of the sauce on each plate. Garnish with additional sauce, and vanilla ice cream, if desired.

Cheesecake Wraps

SERVES 8 TO 10

Another tasty treat that can be made with phyllo dough, this wrap surrounds a cheesecake filling and is topped with cherries or your favorite cheesecake topping. These take only a few minutes to bake and the results are little bites that make a great ending to any meal. I like to vary the toppings, to create a tiled effect when the desserts are placed on the serving tray.

$^1/_2$ POUND PHYLLO DOUGH

1 CUP (2 STICKS) BUTTER, MELTED AND COOLED

$^1/_2$ CUP CINNAMON GRAHAM CRACKER OR VANILLA WAFER CRUMBS

3 PACKAGES (8-OUNCE) CREAM CHEESE, SOFTENED

1 CUP SUGAR

4 EGGS

$1^1/_2$ TEASPOONS VANILLA EXTRACT

2 CUPS CHERRY PIE FILLING, OR TOPPING OF YOUR CHOICE (USE FRESH STRAWBER-RIES, KIWI, RASPBERRIES, CRUSHED PINEAPPLE, OR ORANGE SEGMENTS)

Preheat the oven to 375°F, and grease 48 muffin cups. Keeping the phyllo covered with a kitchen towel, remove 1 sheet, brush with butter, sprinkle with cookie crumbs, and fold in half lengthwise. Brush again with butter, and sprinkle with crumbs, then cut the phyllo into 4 equal squares, and lay each into a muffin cup, pushing down into the cup to make a nest. Repeat with the remaining dough, until you have 48 prepared cups.

In the large bowl of an electric mixer, beat the cream cheese and sugar until fluffy. Add the eggs, 1 at a time, beating until smooth. Fold in the vanilla, and place $^1/_4$ cup filling into each muffin cup. Bake the cheesecakes for 12 to 15 minutes, or until the phyllo is golden-brown and the filling is set. Allow the cheesecakes to cool, and then top with desired fillings. Refrigerate until ready to serve. The finished cakes (without the filling) can be frozen for up to 2 months. Defrost in the refrigerator overnight, and top with filling before serving.

Leftover dried phyllo dough can be used to make a crumbly topping for baked fruits. Using 4 cups of fruit in a 9" square or round, ovenproof pan, mix the fruit with sugar and cinnamon. Shred the phyllo, or cut it into long strips, and measure out 2 cups. Sprinkle the phyllo over the fruit, then melt $1/2$ cup butter. Pour the butter over the phyllo and sprinkle the top liberally with cinnamon-sugar (1 cup sugar mixed with 1 tablespoon cinnamon). Chopped nuts or raisins are excellent additions, as well. Bake the fruit at 375°F for 30 to 40 minutes, until the phyllo is browned, and the fruit is bubbly.

Chocolate Cannoli

SERVES 8 TO 12

When I was a child, my Italian grandmother would always try to get me to eat cannoli, but I just couldn't stomach the rock-hard candied fruit with which she would fill them. Then one day, with a twinkle in her eye, she said she had made me my own special cannoli. Instead of using candied fruit, she had mixed the ricotta cheese with cocoa powder and added chocolate chips to produce the cannoli of my dreams. The cannoli shells are crispy, and the chocolaty ricotta filling is smooth and creamy, studded with semi-sweet chocolate chips. Cannoli shells are sold in the cookie or baking department of many supermarkets, or they can be purchased from Italian bakeries.

12 CANNOLI SHELLS

1/2 CUP HEAVY CREAM, STIFFLY WHIPPED

2 CUPS RICOTTA CHEESE

2 TABLESPOONS AMARETTO DI SARONNO LIQUEUR

1/2 CUP SUGAR

1/4 CUP COCOA POWDER

1/2 CUP MINI CHOCOLATE CHIPS

SHAVED CHOCOLATE AND TOASTED SLIVERED ALMONDS FOR GARNISH

CONFECTIONER'S SUGAR FOR GARNISH

In a large mixing bowl, fold the whipped cream into the ricotta. Add the Amaretto and cocoa powder. Fold in the chocolate chips. Refrigerate the filling until ready to fill the cannoli. Using a knife, spread some of the filling into each end of the cannoli, pushing the filling toward the middle of the tube. When the tubes are filled, dip each end into the shaved chocolate and/or almonds. Refrigerate the cannoli until ready to serve. (You can usually get away with refrigerating them for up to 1 hour before serving.) Sift confectioner's sugar over the top of the cannoli just before serving. These are also divine served in a pool of Raspberry Sauce (see recipe, page 175).

Cookie Wraps

I have always been fascinated with thin cookie batters that bake in the oven and then can be formed around a rolling pin when they come out of the oven. Although these take a bit of watching, your efforts will be rewarded. The crisp, crackly cookie is the perfect foil for Amaretto Crème Anglaise and cut strawberries, or Easy Chocolate Mousse.

NON-STICK COOKING SPRAY

1/2 CUP (1 STICK) BUTTER

1/4 CUP DARK CORN SYRUP

1/3 CUP BROWN SUGAR

3/4 CUP TOASTED SLIVERED ALMONDS*

1/3 CUP ALL-PURPOSE FLOUR

AMARETTO CRÈME ANGLAISE (RECIPE ON NEXT PAGE)

EASY CHOCOLATE MOUSSE (RECIPE ON PAGE 168)

FRESH STRAWBERRIES FOR GARNISH

SHAVED CHOCOLATE FOR GARNISH

Preheat the oven to 325°F. Line a cookie sheet with aluminum foil, and spray with non-stick cooking spray. Also spray a rolling pin or empty wine bottle to form the cookies when they are removed from the oven. In a saucepan, melt the butter and add the corn syrup and brown sugar, bringing the mixture to a boil. Remove from the heat and add the almonds and flour, stirring with a wooden spoon until smooth. Spoon 4 circles of batter (about 1 tablespoon each) onto the prepared pan, and bake for 8 to 10 minutes. Allow the cookies to cool for 1 to 2 minutes. Working quickly, loosen the cookies with a thin metal spatula, and drape the cookies over the rolling pin or wine bottle. If the cookies cool before you roll them return them to the oven to soften. Allow the cookies to cool over the rolling pin, and store them in an airtight container. (The cookies will keep for several days when stored in this fashion.) Fill each cookie with Amaretto Crème Anglaise or Easy Chocolate Mousse, garnishing with fresh strawberries and shaved chocolate.

*To toast almonds: Line a baking pan with foil and lay the nuts on the foil in a single layer. Bake at 350°F for 15 minutes, stirring frequently to prevent burning.

Amaretto Crème Anglaise

A sinfully rich pastry cream, you can use this to top fresh fruit or to stuff cannoli shells. For an orange flavor, substitute Grand Marnier for the Amaretto, or if you prefer not to use liqueur, substitute $^1/_4$ teaspoon almond extract.

$1^2/_3$ CUPS MILK

$^1/_2$ CUP SUGAR

5 EGG YOLKS

1 TEASPOON VANILLA

$1^1/_2$ CUPS HEAVY CREAM, STIFFLY WHIPPED

$^1/_4$ CUP AMARETTO DI SARONNO LIQUEUR (OR $^1/_4$ TEASPOON ALMOND EXTRACT)

In a 4-cup microwave measuring cup, heat the milk and sugar on high for 2 minutes. In a small bowl, whisk the egg yolks, then slowly add to the milk. Cook uncovered at 50% power for 6 minutes, stirring every 2 minutes, until the sauce is thick. Add the vanilla and refrigerate. When the custard is cooled, fold in the whipped cream and the Amaretto. Refrigerate the pastry cream for up to 2 days.

Easy Chocolate Mousse

Smooth and full of chocolate flavor, this mousse will enhance any dessert, whether it is used to fill and frost a torte, eaten by itself in a champagne glass topped with unsweetened whipped cream, or used to fill cookie wraps. You'll love how easy and adaptable this filling is.

1 CUP SEMISWEET CHOCOLATE CHIPS

2 TABLESPOONS BUTTER

3 EGGS, SEPARATED

1 CUP HEAVY WHIPPING CREAM

1/3 CUP SUGAR

Melt the butter and chocolate over low heat in a small saucepan. Remove the chocolate from the heat and transfer to a glass mixing bowl. Whisk in the egg yolks. In a separate bowl, whip the cream until it is stiff. Beat the egg whites in another bowl, until soft peaks begin to form. Add the sugar 2 tablespoons at a time, until all the sugar is incorporated. Take some of the egg whites and fold them into the chocolate mixture. Fold the remaining egg whites into the chocolate mixture using a balloon whisk. Fold in the whipped cream, cover the bowl with plastic wrap, and refrigerate until ready to use.

Cream Puff/Éclair Wraps

SERVES 6

The French have been wrapping their desserts for years, and the cream puff is one we see most often in our bakeries. Unfortunately, most filled cream puffs have been sitting in the bakery case for quite a while, turning them into a soggy, sorry mouthful. I recommend making the shells ahead of time, and keeping them stored in an airtight container (for up to 8 hours) or freezing until ready to serve. Fillings for puffs could include ice cream (this would make them profiterroles), flavored whipped cream, Crème Anglaise, Easy Chocolate Mousse, or lemon mousse. Fill the puffs just before serving.

The only difference between an éclair and a cream puff is the shape of the dough when it is baked. a pastry bag to pipe out the éclairs and an ordinary tablespoon to shape the puffs.

1 CUP WATER

6 (¾ STICK) TABLESPOONS BUTTER

⅛ TEASPOON SALT

1 TABLESPOON SUGAR

1 CUP FLOUR

5 LARGE EGGS

EGG GLAZE: 1 EGG BEATEN WITH 1 TEA-SPOON WATER

CHOICE OF FILLING(S)

CONFECTIONER'S SUGAR, FUDGE SAUCE, OR COCOA POWDER FOR GARNISH

In a heavy, 3-quart saucepan, bring the water and butter to a boil. As soon as the butter is melted, remove the pan from the heat and add the salt, sugar, and flour, and stir with a heavy wooden spoon. Working quickly, add the eggs one at a time, incorporating them totally. The dough will just hold its shape.

While the dough is still warm, preheat the oven to 425°F. Prepare baking sheets by lining them with foil or parchment. Using a tablespoon, form small puffs that are about 1 inch high and 2 inches wide. Space the puffs about 2 inches apart on the cookie sheets.

Brush the puffs with the egg glaze, being careful to keep the glaze on the top of the puffs. Bake for 20 minutes, until the puffs are doubled in size and golden-brown. They should be crisp to the touch. Turn off the oven and remove the puffs. Slit each puff in the side (to release some of the steam), and return to the oven for another 5 minutes. Cool the puffs on wire racks. Store in airtight containers or freeze for up to 1 month.

To form éclairs, use a pastry bag fitted with a plain tip. Pipe out 3-inch-by-1-inch cylinders onto a prepared cookie sheet. Bake at 425°F for 25 minutes, slit, and leave in the turned-off oven for 5 additional minutes.

To fill éclairs or puffs, cut off the tops and spoon in the filling. Or, using a filled pastry bag, poke a hole in the lower third of the pastry and fill with desired cream. Refrigerate after filling. Sprinkle the tops with confectioner's sugar, fudge sauce, or confectioner's sugar mixed with cocoa.

Gorilla Wraps

Frozen bananas have been a mainstay at ice-cream stands for years. Simple to make, they keep a long time in the freezer. You can have these treats wrapped and ready for your crew when they sit down to watch their favorite video.

6 LARGE FIRM BANANAS (MAKE SURE THEY ARE NOT BRUISED), PEELED

2 CUPS SEMISWEET CHOCOLATE CHIPS

2 TABLESPOONS BUTTER

1 CUP CHOPPED PEANUTS

Cut each banana into 4 to 5 chunks (each about 2 inches long). Place the bananas on a foil-lined cookie sheet and freeze for about 20 minutes. Meanwhile, melt the chocolate with the butter in a saucepan or in the microwave for 2 minutes on high power. When the chocolate is melted, whisk it until it is smooth and has cooled slightly. Using a skewer, dip the bananas into the chocolate, using a rubber spatula to make sure that the banana is completely coated. Place the peanuts on a cookie sheet lined with foil and roll the banana chunks in the peanuts. Place the finished pieces on a foil-lined cookie sheet and freeze for 1 hour. Remove from the freezer and store in airtight containers, then return to the freezer. When ready to serve, allow the wraps to sit out for 2 to 4 minutes to defrost.

Peach Praline Purses

Peaches and pecans team up for a delicious dessert combination when wrapped in phyllo dough and served with a Praline Sauce. These pastries can be wrapped 2 days ahead of time, or frozen for up to 1 month.

4 CUPS SLICED PEELED PEACHES, FRESH OR FROZEN, DEFROSTED

3/4 CUP GRANULATED SUGAR

2 TABLESPOONS CORNSTARCH

1/4 CUP BROWN SUGAR

1/2 CUP CHOPPED PECANS

1/2 POUND PHYLLO DOUGH

1 CUP (2 STICKS) BUTTER, MELTED AND COOLED

1/2 CUP CINNAMON GRAHAM CRACKER CRUMBS OR VANILLA WAFER CRUMBS

PRALINE SAUCE (RECIPE ON NEXT PAGE)

Combine the peaches, sugar, and cornstarch in a large mixing bowl, tossing to coat the peaches. Let the peaches stand at room temperature for 1 hour. Combine the brown sugar and pecans in a small bowl. Lay the phyllo out on a flat work surface. Cover with a kitchen towel. Remove 1 sheet of phyllo and brush all over with melted butter and sprinkle with cookie crumbs. Repeat with a second sheet of phyllo. Fold the phyllo in half lengthwise, brushing with additional butter and sprinkling with crumbs. Using a slotted spoon, drain about 1/3 cup of peaches and arrange them in the center of the phyllo. Then sprinkle with 1 tablespoon of the pecans. Taking the opposite corners, draw all four corners into the center, twisting the top of the phyllo into a knot. Drizzle with additional melted butter. Using a wide spatula, transfer the phyllo to a cookie sheet lined with aluminum foil. When ready to bake, preheat the oven to 400°F, and bake the wraps for 20 minutes, or until golden-brown. The Peach Purses can be refrigerated before baking for 2 days or frozen up to one month. Serve garnished with chopped pecans and Praline Sauce.

Praline Sauce

Smooth, studded with pecans, and just a hint of Bourbon, this sauce is perfect with the Peach Praline Purses.

6 TABLESPOONS (³/₄ STICK) BUTTER

1¹/₂ CUPS PECAN HALVES

1¹/₂ CUPS GRANULATED SUGAR

³/₄ CUP BROWN SUGAR

¹/₂ CUP MILK

1 TEASPOON BOURBON (OR YOU MAY SUBSTITUTE VANILLA EXTRACT)

Melt the butter in a 2-quart saucepan. Add the pecan halves, stirring for 2 minutes over medium heat. Add the sugars, and cook until they are melted. Gradually add the milk and Bourbon, bringing the mixture to a boil for 1 minute. Remove from the heat and serve immediately, or refrigerate for up to 3 weeks. Reheat the sauce over low heat, until warm.

Poached Pear Wraps

The ultimate in sinful seductive desserts, pears are poached in vanilla syrup, chilled, then covered in warm bittersweet chocolate, and served in a pool of Raspberry Sauce. The pears can be poached 2 days ahead of time, then refrigerated in their syrup. The sauces can both be made ahead of time. The Bittersweet Chocolate Sauce should be warmed just before serving.

6 RIPE PEARS

4 CUPS WATER

2 TEASPOONS LEMON ZEST

2 TABLESPOONS FRESH LEMON JUICE

1 VANILLA BEAN, CUT IN HALF (OR SUBSTITUTE 1 TABLESPOON VANILLA POWDER)

1 1/2 CUPS SUGAR

Peel the pears and, using a melon baller, core the pears from the bottom. Place the pears in a 4-quart saucepan and add the remaining ingredients to the pan. Bring the water to a simmer, then cook, uncovered, for 6 to 8 minutes, or until the pears are tender when tested with a sharp knife. If you plan to use the pears immediately, remove them from the syrup to drain. Otherwise, the pears can be left in the syrup and refrigerated for up to 4 days.

Powdered vanilla is available in the baking section of your local grocers. You can use it in place of vanilla extract or vanilla beans. See Source Guide, page 183.

Bittersweet Chocolate Sauce

Smooth, silky, and out of this world. You will also enjoy this sauce over ice cream, cream puffs, and éclairs.

¹/₂ CUP (1 STICK) BUTTER	1¹/₂ CUPS SUGAR
4 OUNCES BITTERSWEET CHOCOLATE	1 CUP HEAVY CREAM

In a small saucepan, melt the butter with the chocolate. Stir in the sugar, and add the heavy cream, whisking until smooth. Remove from the heat. Store in an airtight container in the refrigerator. Reheat to serve.

Raspberry Sauce

4 CUPS FRESH OR FROZEN RASPBERRIES	1 CUP SUGAR
2 TEASPOONS FRESH LEMON JUICE	

Combine the ingredients in a small saucepan and bring to a boil. Simmer for 3 minutes, stirring constantly. Taste the sauce and correct for sweetness by adding additional sugar if necessary. Strain the sauce through a fine sieve. Refrigerate in an airtight container.

ASSEMBLY

RASPBERRY SAUCE	UNSWEETENED WHIPPED CREAM AND TWISTS OF LEMON PEEL FOR GARNISH (OPTIONAL)
POACHED PEARS (AT ROOM TEMPERATURE)	
BITTERSWEET CHOCOLATE SAUCE	

Swirl 2 or 3 tablespoons of the Raspberry Sauce onto each dessert plate. Center a pear in the sauce, and top with warmed Bittersweet Chocolate Sauce. If desired, you may serve the pears garnished with unsweetened whipped cream and twists of lemon peel.

Pumpkin Hazelnut Wraps

SERVES 8 TO 10

My favorite Thanksgiving dessert is an ice cream pie using this delectable pumpkin ice cream filling. But when I had thirty guests coming for dinner one Thanksgiving, I decided to roll the ice cream filling into balls, then coat with the crust ingredients, and freeze until dinner. These are wonderful to have on hand for unexpected guests, and the sauce adds a special touch to an otherwise spectacular dessert.

1/2 CUP (1 STICK) BUTTER, MELTED

6 TABLESPOONS GRANULATED SUGAR

2 CUPS CINNAMON GRAHAM CRACKER CRUMBS

1 CUP GROUND HAZELNUTS

1 CAN (16-OUNCE) PUMPKIN PUREE

2/3 CUP BROWN SUGAR

1 TEASPOON GROUND CINNAMON

1/2 TEASPOON GROUND NUTMEG

1 TEASPOON GROUND GINGER

1/8 TEASPOON GROUND CLOVES

3 PINTS VANILLA ICE CREAM

BUTTERSCOTCH SAUCE (RECIPE ON NEXT PAGE)

MINT LEAVES AND WHIPPED CREAM FOR GARNISH

In a small mixing bowl, combine the butter, sugar, graham cracker crumbs, and hazelnuts. Stir to combine, then refrigerate while making the pumpkin filling.

In a 2-quart saucepan, heat the pumpkin with the brown sugar and the spices. Refrigerate the pumpkin mixture until cold. Soften the ice cream, and beat it into the pumpkin mixture. If the filling is too runny, freeze for one hour before shaping. Using a large ice cream scoop, form the filling into balls 2 inches in diameter. Roll in the hazelnut crumbs, place on a cookie sheet that has been lined with foil or parchment paper. Freeze until firm, then store in zipper-type freezer bags. When ready to serve, swirl some of the hot Butterscotch Sauce onto a dessert plate. Place 1 pumpkin ball on each dessert plate, and garnish with mint leaves and a rosette of whipped cream.

Butterscotch Sauce

4 TABLESPOONS (½ STICK) BUTTER   1 CUP HEAVY CREAM

1 CUP BROWN SUGAR

Melt the butter with the brown sugar, stirring with a wooden spoon until the sugar melts. Add the cream and stir until the sauce boils. Remove the sauce from the heat and serve immediately. The sauce will keep refrigerated for up to 2 weeks. Reheat before serving.

Raspberry Napoleon Wraps

SERVES 6 TO 8

One of my favorite bakeries makes a chocolate Napoleon that breaks apart when you bite into it. The filling is not too sweet and is flavored beautifully with raspberries. I've taken their idea and gone over the edge, by wrapping the puff pastry around raspberry preserves and chocolate ganache, then garnishing with sweetened whipped cream. I will warn you that you'll dream about these once you've made them. The puff pastry wrap can be baked the day you would like to serve it, the ganache keeps in the refrigerator for several days, and I recommend that you assemble these right before serving.

1 17¼-OUNCE PACKAGE FROZEN PUFF PASTRY

½ CUP SUGAR

8 OUNCES BITTERSWEET CHOCOLATE, CHOPPED

1¾ CUPS HEAVY WHIPPING CREAM

½ CUP SEEDLESS RASPBERRY JAM

1 CUP FRESH RASPBERRIES

CONFECTIONER'S SUGAR FOR TOPPING

Line a jelly-roll pan with foil or parchment and preheat the oven to 425°F. Roll out the puff pastry sheets, using the sugar as you would flour to roll it. The dough should measure 12 × 16 inches. Cut the dough in half, then cut each half into 4 equal parts. Place the dough onto the prepared pan. Repeat with the remaining dough. Bake the wraps for 15 to 20 minutes, or until they are golden-brown. Remove from the oven and allow to cool. When cool, store in airtight containers for up to 1 day. Recrisp in a 400-degree oven for 4 minutes several hours before serving.

Prepare the ganache. Melt the chocolate with ³/₄ cup of the heavy cream. Allow the mixture to cool. Whip the remaining cream until stiff peaks appear. Add the ganache to the whipped cream, whisking until combined. Refrigerate until ready to serve.

To serve, spread 1 tablespoon raspberry jam over one piece of pastry. Cover with ¹/₄ cup of ganache, some fresh raspberries, topping with a second piece of pastry dough. Sprinkle the tops with confectioner's sugar before serving. If you would like to assemble the Napoleons ahead of time, they may be refrigerated for up to 2 hours.

Tuxedo-Wrapped Strawberries

SERVES 8

Enrobed in white and dark chocolates, these luscious strawberries are dressed for a formal occasion. Dipping the strawberries takes no time at all and the results are spectacular. Make sure to dry the strawberries thoroughly before dipping, and to leave them at room temperature after they are dipped. If you must refrigerate them, they will sweat when you remove them from the cold. Wipe with a dry paper towel just before serving.

2 CUPS WHITE CHOCOLATE, CUT INTO SMALL PIECES

2 CUPS SEMISWEET CHOCOLATE, CUT INTO SMALL PIECES

24 PERFECT 2-INCH STRAWBERRIES WITH STEMS, WASHED AND PATTED DRY

Cut 2 sheets of waxed paper or parchment the length plus 4 inches longer than a cookie sheet or jelly-roll pan. Microwave the white chocolate at 70% power for 90 seconds. Stir with a wooden spoon and continue to cook for up to 3 additional minutes. Remove from the microwave. Holding a strawberry by the stem, either dip it into the white chocolate or drizzle white chocolate off a spoon to coat the berry all the way up to the stem. Lay the berry on the parchment and continue to dip the remaining strawberries. Lay the other piece of parchment onto a cookie sheet or jelly-roll pan. Heat the semisweet chocolate in the same way, and remove it from the microwave. Dip the strawberries in a similar manner, leaving a $1/2$-inch rim of white chocolate peeking out from under the dark chocolate. Lay these strawberries onto the second sheet of waxed paper. Allow to stand at room temperature for up to 3 hours. (If you need to refrigerate the strawberries, they will keep for 8 hours.) The berries can be served by themselves, or as a garnish for ice cream, chocolate mousse, or as cake decorations.

Volcanic Hawaiian Wraps

A flaming taste of the islands is poured over folded crêpes to create a delicate ending to any meal. Feel free to substitute other tropical fruits and nuts, and if you are anxious about flaming the crêpes, omit the rum.

Dessert Crêpes

¹/₂ CUP ALL-PURPOSE FLOUR	1 TABLESPOON BUTTER, MELTED
1 LARGE EGG	1 TABLESPOON SUGAR
¹/₂ CUP MILK	NON-STICK COOKING SPRAY

Place the flour in a deep bowl. Combine the egg, milk, butter, and sugar in another bowl, and whisk together until smooth. Gradually pour the egg mixture over the flour, blending until smooth. (A food processor or immersion blender works very well here.) Refrigerate the batter for at least 1 hour.

Preheat an 8- to 10-inch nonstick skillet or crêpe pan. Spray the pan with non-stick cooking spray. Pour in a thin film of batter, tilting the pan to cover the bottom. When small bubbles appear on the surface of the crêpe, lift the edge, and turn the crêpe over. Cook until the crêpe is firm. Remove the crêpe to a plate, and stack the crêpes between waxed paper. The crêpes can be refrigerated overnight or frozen in zipper-type freezer bags for one month. Defrost overnight in the refrigerator.

Volcanic Filling

1 MEDIUM PINEAPPLE, PEELED, CORED,
AND CHOPPED INTO $^1/_2$-INCH PIECES

$^1/_2$ CUP (1 STICK) BUTTER

$^1/_2$ CUP BROWN SUGAR

$^1/_2$ TEASPOON GROUND CINNAMON

DASH OF GRATED NUTMEG

1 CUP CHOPPED MACADAMIA NUTS

$^1/_4$ CUP MYERS'S DARK RUM

$^1/_2$ CUP FLAKED COCONUT (OPTIONAL)

In a 12-inch skillet, melt the butter and add the sugar, cinnamon, nutmeg, and macadamia nuts. Sauté over medium heat until the nuts become coated with the butter/sugar mixture. Add the pineapple, and continue to stir the mixture until coated. Fold each crêpe into quarters and arrange 2 on each dessert plate. Reheat the sauce and when the sauce comes to a boil, add the rum. If it does not ignite on its own, light a match to it, taking care to stand away from the pan. Shake the pan until the flames go out. Pour $^1/_4$ cup of sauce over the crêpes. Top the crêpes with flaked coconut, if desired. If you are serving a large group, you can arrange the crêpes in a 13 × 9-inch baking dish, and refrigerate the crêpes and sauce until ready to use. Reheat the sauce, pour over the crêpes, and bake in a 350-degree oven for 20 minutes.

Source Guide

If you live in an area with limited availability, here are a few sources that you can write to find out how to obtain their products.

Athens Pastries and Frozen Foods, Inc.
13600 Snow Road
Cleveland, Ohio 44142
Phyllo dough

Babylon Bakery
11693 Sheldon Street
Unit 2
Sun Valley, California 91352
818-767-6076
Lavosh

Boyajian, Inc.
385 California Street
Newton, Massachusetts 02160
617-527-6677
Flavored oils, smoked salmon, caviar

Cook Flavoring Company
P.O. Box 890
Tacoma, Washington 98401
206-627-5499
Powdered vanilla and other flavorings

Frieda's, Inc.
4465 Corporate Center Drive
Los Alamitos, California 90720
714-826-6100
Web site: http://www.friedas.com
Purveyors of unusual food stuffs, notably vegetables, and fruits and fresh crêpes.

The Green House
P.O. Box 231069
Encinitas, California 92023-1069
619-942-5371
Dehydrated herbs

Joyce Chen Products, Inc.
6 Fortune Drive
Billerica, Massachusetts 01821
508-671-9500
Gyoza Press and fine Asian products, including sauces, and equipment

King Arthur Flour
P.O. Box 876
Norwich, Vermont 05055
800-777-4434
Baking equipment, exceptional flours and grains, spices, oils, and unusual ingredients. Have them send you a catalogue—you'll be hooked!

Mr. Pita
5200 S. Alameda Street
Vernon, California 90058
Pita bread

Pepperidge Farm, Inc.
Norwalk, Connecticut 06856
1-800-762-8301
Frozen puff pastry dough

SAF Instant Yeast
400 South Fourth Street
Suite 310
Minneapolis, Minnesota 55415
800-641-4615
Absolutely the best yeast on the market—it never fails!

Williams-Sonoma
P.O. Box 7456
San Francisco, California 94120-7456
800-541-2233
An incredible catalogue and stores with just about anything you could want to make anything edible!

Sample Menus

Now that you have all these wonderful recipes for dynamite wraps, how do you put it all together to make a special meal, or turn dinner into an event? Here are a few sample menus that you can use to build an occasion for wrapping up a fabulous dinner.

Tour of the Orient

CHICKEN AND VEGETABLE GYOZA

GORILLA WRAPS

BEIJING CITY CHICKEN WRAPPED IN
LETTUCE LEAVES

Pacific Rim Dinner

ORIENTAL CHICKEN AND SPINACH WRAPS

VOLCANIC HAWAIIAN WRAPS

PEKING DUCK WRAPS

Mediterranean Madness

PROSCIUTTO PALMIERS

CHICKEN AND RED POTATO WRAPS

TOMATO, CUCUMBER, AND FETA PITAS

CHOCOLATE CANNOLI

Italian Vegetarian Dinner

PARMESAN BRUSCHETTA

EGGPLANT WRAPS

GRILLED MARINATED VEGGIE WRAPS

CAPPUCCINO WRAPS

Summer Luncheon or Dinner

CALIFORNIA ROLLS

LAYERED VEGGIE WRAPS

PEACH PRALINE PURSES

CUCUMBER WRAPS

ROAST BEEF AND STILTON WRAPS

COOKIE WRAPS

Elegant Meals for the Boss

PROSCIUTTO-WRAPPED STRAWBERRIES

HOT SPINACH SALAD WRAP

STEAK AND GARLIC MASHED POTATOES
WRAPS

PUMPKIN HAZELNUT WRAPS

SPANAKOPITAS

FRUIT AND CHEESE WRAPS

PESTO SWORDFISH WRAPS

TUXEDO WRAPPED STRAWBERRIES

Beautiful Brunches

WRAPPED BRIE WITH APRICOTS AND DRIED
CRANBERRIES

BREAKFAST STRUDELS

BANANAS FOSTERS' WRAPS

JICAMA STICKS

OMELETTE WRAPS

CAPPUCCINO WRAPS

Vegetarian Delights

CURRIED MUSHROOM ROLLS

EGG DILL AND TOMATO SALAD WRAPS

BROCCOLI, MUSHROOM, AND CHEESE
CALZONE OR PIZZA WRAPS

COOKIE WRAPS

SPANAKOPITAS

BULGUR WHEAT SALAD WRAPS

RATATOUILLE CREPES

ALMOND CINNAMON PALMIERS

South of the Border Fiestas

MEXICANA TORTILLA ROLLS

BLACK BEAN, CORN, AND SALSA WRAP

FISH TACOS ESPECIAL

COOKIE WRAPS

BASIL WRAPPED SCALLOP SEVICHE

BLACK BEAN, CORN, AND SALSA WRAP

COCO LOCO QUESADILLA OR QUESADILLA
MERCEDES

TUXEDO-WRAPPED STRAWBERRIES

Index

Grilled
fish tacos especial, 107–108
meat fajitas, 91
veggie (marinated) wraps, 70–71
Guacamole, 39
Gyoza, chicken and vegetable, 26–27

Ham and asparagus wraps with cucumber
Hollandaise, 98–99
Hard-cooked eggs, 66
Hawaiian volcano wraps, 180–181
Hazelnut pumpkin wraps, 176
Herbs, fresh vs. dried, 16
Hot spinach salad wraps, 68

Ingredients, storing, 15–18, 58
Italian
roll-ups, 32
vegetarian dinner menu, 188

Jammin' PB&J wraps, 33
Jasmine rice, 120–121
Jicama sticks, 34
Johnnycakes with smoked salmon and
capers, 35–36

Kebab wraps, 109–110
Kimchee American style, 113–114
Korean beef rolls, 112–114

Lavosh, 3
Layered veggie wraps, 69
Leafy green vegetables, 5, 58
Leftover hints, 77
phyllo dough, 164
puff pastry, 46
roast beef and Stilton wrap, 72
tortillas, 38

Leftover hints (cont.)
turkey dinner wraps, 125
Lemon, 69
dill magnesia, 139
zest, 110
Lettuce leaves, Beijing City chicken
wrapped in, 83
Lowering fat, hint, 2

Mango
salsa, 116
snapper wraps, 115
Marinated grilled veggie wraps, 70–71
Mashed potato and garlic with steak
wraps, 147–148
Magnesia, lemon dill, 139
Meals under wraps, 77–153
Meat (grilled) fajitas, 91
Mediterranean madness dinner, 188
Menus, 187–190
Mexicana tortilla rolls, 37
Mousse (chocolate) for cookie wraps, 168
Mushroom
bacon, tomato filling for omelette wraps,
118
broccoli, and cheese calzone, 89–90
rolls, curried, 31
shiitake Merlot sauce, 148

Napolean with raspberry wraps, 178
Nori, 5

Omelette wraps, 117–119
Oriental chicken and spinach wraps,
40–41
Orzo, shrimp, and sun-dried tomato
wraps, 74